# Introduction

A 'Topic' is an approach to teaching in a Primary School which involves various apparently unrelated tasks being carried out under the umbrella of a common title or theme such as 'Anglo-Saxon Britain'.

Topic work always:

- **includes class, group and individual work with some element of choice.**
- **involves practical activities.**
- **uses themes selected which are thought appropriate to the interests and stage of development of the children involved.**
- **involves first hand experiences such as a visit or visitors.**
- **involves some sort of investigation.**
- **involves information gathering skills.**
- **crosses some curriculum boundaries.**
  **It should also include, if possible, an element of FUN.**

The purpose of this book is to provide a bank of ideas and photocopiable activities, based on the study of Anglo-Saxon Britain, which fulfil the above criteria. It is envisaged that a busy class teacher will use his or her professional judgement to select activities appropriate to their own individual situation.

Topical Resources publishes a range of Educational Materials for use in Primary Schools and Pre-School Nurseries and Playgroups.

**For latest catalogue:**

**Tel: 01772 863158**

**Fax: 01772 866153**

**E.Mail: sales@topical-resources.co.uk**

**For free sample pages, visit our website on:**

**www.topical-resources.co.uk**

Copyright © 2005 Paul Cross

Illustrated by John Hutchinson

Printed in Great Britain for 'Topical Resources', Publishers of Educational Materials, P.O. Box 329, Broughton, Preston. PR3 5LT by T. Snape & Company Ltd., Boltons Court, Preston.

Typeset by Artworks, 69 Worden Lane, Leyland, Lancashire. PR5 2BD Tel: 01772 431010

First Published Jan 2005
ISBN 1 872977 88 X

# Contents

# Notes for Teachers

# Background Information for Class Lessons

## The Origins and Traditions of the Anglo-Saxons

Before they came to England, the peoples who we know as the Anglo-Saxons lived in the region of present day north western Germany and eastern Holland. As they had no written history, we have two different sources of information about their continental past. Firstly, some of their rich tradition of story telling survived until later on in their settlement in England when they developed a written language. The monks such as Bede of Jarrow wrote down these verbal legends, and some of their folk history as different tribes in their Germanic homelands.

Secondly, we know something of their 'barbaric' past from Roman historians who recorded the traditions of the tribes who were held back on the north eastern frontiers of the Roman Empire.

Bede and other Saxon monks tended to stress the heroic deeds of mighty leaders in their warfare with other tribes, much in the style of the well known Anglo-Saxon poem Beowulf. From these writings we know of such things as the tradition of Wergild, when a person injured in some conflict with other tribes would seek revenge through a code of revenge payments and forfeits.

From both the Roman historians and from the later Anglo-Saxon monks we can read about the Germanic tradition of inheritance, where the land of a thane or tribal leader was split between his male heirs. Generations of this practice meant that the people had less and less land. This in turn led to frequent inter-tribal warfare, and a constant cutting down of large tracts of forest on the western frontiers of the territories which bordered the Roman Empire. This points to a pressure on the people of these areas of Germany and Holland around 400 to 200 B.C., a pressure to find more land, more living space. Roman writers such as Pliny, Tacitus and Ptolemy frequently report the raids by German tribes on settlements along the Rhine. These are portrayed as wild attempts to grab land and bring down the local Roman garrisons. The barbarous nature of the tribes of the area is constantly highlighted in order to raise the profile of retaining ever growing numbers of Roman legions on the empire's north eastern perimeter to hold back these barbaric tribes.

The main tribes which Saxon historians like Bede, writing about three hundred years after the events, identify as taking part in these raids were the Anglii, the Jutae, and the Saxonii. Many of these tribes began to act in confederation to be better able to gain new lands and beat the disciplined fighting force of the Roman legions.

## Migration Leads to Invasion and Settlement

Raiding parties began to use ships to move steadily more westward from modern day Fresia, Jutland, and the Netherlands. Eventually these raids moved from attacking the northern coast of the Roman colonies of Gaul (France), across the Channel and started to raid the rich Roman colony of Britain. There were other reasons for targeting Roman Britain, for the south eastern frontiers of the Roman Empire were being pushed steadily westwards as wave upon wave of wildly barbaric Goths, Visigoths and Vandals pushed for more and more land. Under such pressure the Roman Emperor called the legions back to defend Rome. The Anglo-Saxons would be aware of this from captives taken during their attacks on Gaul. Certainly from about 420 A.D Britain was facing increasing raids and the chiefs or kings of Britain under threat, are feeling vulnerable to the raiders from across the channel. Bede places a date of 449 for the invitation

from Vortigern, a Romano-British King of Kent, to a famed Saxon fighting thane Hengst and his brother Horsa to bring their men to fight for the Roman Britons against the Anglii raiders. While Horsa was killed in a battle between Germanic raiders and the Germanic mercenaries, Hengst triumphed. He went on to fight many more battles until he turned on the Britons, defeated them in a fierce battle and made Kent an Anglo-Saxon Kingdom, driving the Britons out to London and territories to the west. Whilst the actual dates are merely the estimation of an historian writing three hundred years after the events, the story of the invaders, mercenaries and threatened defenders create an atmosphere of chaos in a threatened island, and of stronger, hungrier invaders making settlement space for their peoples. But all this was in the small area of present day Kent to the south and east of the Medway. This was merely the start of a process that was to last for around 300 years.

## The Pattern of the Anglo-Saxon Invasions of Britain

It is vital to stress that the Britain of 450 A.D. was not suddenly overnight changed from being a land ruled by Romano-British leaders to the rule of Anglo-Saxon kings. The Anglli, the Jutae and the Saxonii appear in themselves to have been loose confederations formed by thanes from different settlements, within the geographical area delineated above, joining together for mutual protection or advancement. When these separate thanes decided with their people to venture on a raid on Britain their motives could be mixed between a desire for plunder, for gold, silver and precious goods to add aggrandisement to the thane, and through him his people: or to gain richer and larger land holding for the thane and his people. This would raise the stature of the thane and his tribe. The thane would attain the highest honour that these Germanic tribes could grant to a leader when the leader was seen as the great benefactor and wonderful provider for his people.

Thus the Anglo-Saxon raids and following settlements were very spasmodic, they happened over a long period of time following 450 A.D. Historians used to theorise that the Jutes settled Kent and the London area, that differing groups of Saxonii settled in Sussex, Wessex and Essex. The Anglii made their homelands in East Anglia and Northumbria, whilst Mercia was settled later by different groups of all the invading tribes. Modern historical research points to there being a more spasmodic settlement of all tribes in a very mixed way throughout England. The five major and separate kingdoms of Northumbria, Mercia, Anglia, Kent, and Essex only emerge later in the settlement of the Anglo-Saxons.

## A Typical Anglo-Saxon Settlement

The Anglo-Saxons had lived in tribal clan villages in their Germanic homelands so when they came to Britain they tended to form similar tribal units. A typical early Anglo-Saxon settlement would have a large wooden Hall for the thane and his family and servants or slaves, around this would be clustered very simple thatched roof one room cottages. Many of these, evidence shows, had a below ground level pit covered by a thatched roof. The tribal settlement was normally near a water source, on an easily defended site, surrounded by a defensive moat outside a palisade fence or raised bank surmounted by a fence. At first all the buildings were of wood as this was readily available, indeed forest clearing was a general settlement pattern for the Anglo-Saxons. Another pattern was to take over a Celtic

# Background Information for Class Lessons

Romano-British village in battle, enslave the surviving populace and expand the new village through forest or woodland clearance. Many of these early wooden settlements would, through time, be rebuilt in stone where such material was locally available. As the thane who headed a settlement became more powerful so would his village expand to township status. From early in the last century historians held as almost a dogma that Anglo-Saxon settlement of Britain was village based, they portrayed little Anglo-Saxon take over of the Roman towns and cities of Britain. Modern archaeological research shows that the Anglo-Saxons saw the benefits of an already established fortified site, inside which they could set up their own pattern of settlement. What can safely be agreed however is that the majority of Anglo-Saxon village or town settlements are found to the East of a line from the Tyne to the Mersey, excluding the very Celtic kingdoms of Wales, Devon and Cornwall.

## Anglo-Saxon Society

By the time the Anglo-Saxons had settled in England they already had an established social hierarchy. Local kings, by their command in battle, alliance or judicious marriage, were a great provider of security, bounty and land to their follower thanes. In return, the king, demanded loyalty from his thanes, an instant turn out of his thanes and their people in any dispute for one hundred days. Rewards for success in battle were the cement that held this social structure together, a king being assessed as 'great' by his ability to provide bounty for all ranks of his followers. Great issues for a kingdom or matters of important justice administration would see the king meeting in council with his thanes for a collective decision. Within the king's extended family there was often a fierce rivalry at any succession as any member, even strong minded women with male allies, could claim the throne. Primogeniture was not an Anglo-Saxon concept. There were frequent family feuds at succession time with family murders a frequent event at such a time.

The tribal thane was the next rank in Anglo-Saxon society. His skill in battle, diplomacy, gold collecting and marriage making was crucial to his own aggrandisement and the advancement of his tribe. He was regarded by his tribe as their provider. Their prosperity and security were bound up with their thane's strength in the three areas; battle, alliance making and match making. Total obedience and service was required by a thane from his people, punishment for any disobedience was brutal and harsh. A wrong done to the tribe either by a tribal member or an enemy had a price; a limb lost would be repaid by the same loss inflicted on the perpetrator of the first wrong as a savage act of vengeance. A promise broken could lead to the hand that had made the deal being chopped off in retribution. In matters of succession to any thane, the procedures described for Saxon royal families applied. The women-folk of the king's and thane's families led lives of comparative leisure with sewing, care of the children, hawking and hunting and command of the domestic arrangements in the tribal hall their only occupations. Many women of these classes became nuns or abbesses in the Christian monasteries that prospered in later Anglo-Saxon times.

Below the thane were his churls. They held land from their thane in return for service on the thane's land and for turning out at the thane's bidding for warfare, vengeance raids or defence. The churls were farmers, many of whom also had a trade that was useful to the tribe. The churls and their families would receive bounty from their leader in relation to their worth to the thane when a battle, alliance or marriage brought benefit to the tribe. Churls had to follow their thane into any battle or campaign the king demanded, but their service on the king's part was limited to one hundred days so that the farmer churls would not lose too much by their absence from their farms. The wives and women-folk of the churls were partners in all the farming work of their men-folk, as well as being the cook, child minder and crafts-women in making and repairing clothes. It was only in battle service that they didn't follow their men. However, they were then in sole charge of the farming operations when the men were away.

Below the churls in the social structure in Anglo-Saxon society were the freemen and women. They were labourers and servants. Their lives were controlled by churls and thanes. They could aspire through hard graft or reward for a special deed to become churls, though this elevation was rare. Below the freemen and women were the slaves, often captives from a rival tribe or kingdom. Their lives could be dispensed with by a whim from their owner. Their lives were full of hard manual work, harsh treatment and often brutal early deaths.

## The Beliefs and Gods of the Anglo-Saxons

The Anglo-Saxons were worshippers of natural phenomena. Ancient trees, springs, waterfalls and some lakes were considered magical and mystical. They believed that elves, sprites and gnomic creatures lived in these places and that they could bring good or evil fortune. Evidence from the burials at Sutton Hoo in East Anglia show a belief in life after death, and of the need for the dead to have useful objects with them for their journey after death. Other Anglo-Saxon burials have cremated ashes in bowls or urns, occasionally with grave goods for the after life.

First amongst the gods worshipped by the Anglo-Saxons was Woden, who often appeared in the guise of a raven, a snake or a wild boar. Most Anglo-Saxon kings liked to claim descent from Woden for his power and cunning as founder of the Germanic people. Woden's wife Frig was the goddess of fertility, of seed time and harvest. It was to her that the Anglo-Saxons looked to ensure a bountiful food supply. Thor was worshipped as the god of the sky, his thunder and lightening were feared. He was the one to whom the Anglo-Saxons prayed about the weather they wanted for any project. Tiw was the battle god portrayed as a raven, an eagle or wild boar. His blessing would ensure victory over any foe. That the Anglo-Saxon pagan gods were close to their people is witnessed by the fact that their names give us four day's names in our calendar now.

## The Anglo-Saxons and Christianity

Many of the Romano-British people, who lived in Britain before the Anglo-Saxons raided or settled in Britain, were Christians. For many years following the Anglo-Saxon invasions Christianity was wiped out, or driven with the remnants of the Romano-British people into the Celtic fringes of Wales, Devon and Cornwall.

Around 590 A.D., Pope Gregory in Rome met with some Anglo-Saxon captives from Gaul. The youths had become Christians due to their captor's preaching and begged Gregory to send missionaries to convert Britain. Gregory sent Augustine with a party of monks to Britain. We know of Augustine's conversions of the Kentish king and people and the establishment of his seat or Cathedral at Canterbury mainly from his letters to Pope

# Background Information for Class Lessons

Gregory, which detail the conversions and spread of Christianity from Augustine's landing in 597. The new religion had periods when it seemed to spread and take over kingdoms like East Anglia, Mercia and Northumbria only for a sympathetic king to die and the new king swing back to the old Germanic forms of worship. It was after such a swing back in Northumbria that Oswald, returning as king from his exile in Iona brought Irish monks from Iona under the tough leadership of St. Aidan to the mission and monastery at Lindisfarne. Trained in the tough muscular Christianity of Ireland with its richness of scholarship and book production, Aidan and his successor Cuthbert were able to found churches monasteries and cathedrals through much of Britain. The twin Roman and Irish based Christian missions meant that by the end of the Anglo-Saxon period there were over 150 monasteries for monks and nuns in England. These came to be seats of great learning in Biblical, saintly and secular studies. A vast part of what we know of the Anglo-Saxon peoples comes from historical writings carried out in a large number of these monasteries. The Irish church had long been a source of knowledge, teaching, art and literature in Europe sending missionaries and teachers throughout northern Europe. The Anglo-Saxon monasteries carried on this fine tradition sending missionaries like Boniface, Anselm and Alcuin to create many dioceses in the old Germanic homeland of the Anglo-Saxons.

## Offa a Great Anglo-Saxon Figure

With six major kingdoms and around five hundred years of Anglo-Saxon dominance of England it is little wonder that great figures stand out as rulers from this period. Their strengths came from typical old Anglo-Saxon core values such as their prowess in battle, cunning in forming alliances, with the added new factor an encouragement of learning and the arts and a championing of the Christian faith. Offa, King of Mercia from 757 to 796, was just such a king. He fought battles throughout Anglo-Saxon Britain conquering large parts of Northumbria, East Anglia and Wessex until 774 when he claimed the title of 'King of all the English.' When a king of Anglia opposed him, Offa rode into the king's city, captured the king and personally beheaded him for daring to stand against his power. He married off his daughters to the Kings of Northumbria, East Anglia and Kent, thereby receiving their allegiance. The great Holy Roman Emperor Charlemagne sent him presents to mark their countries' trade ties. The Pope made one of Offa's bishops an archbishop, the only time there was a third archbishop in England apart from York and Canterbury. His building of the one hundred and fifty mile earth wall and ditch which bears his name shows the power and organisational skills of the man. His value of art and crafts are shown in the magnificent coins that survive from his reign. Found throughout England, these coins in gold and silver are recognised as the finest examples of metalwork for the whole period. This is almost all that is known of the enigmatic Offa one of the most powerful and longest reigning of all Anglo-Saxon kings.

## The Viking Hordes Terrify the Anglo-Saxons

Suddenly in 793, a terrifying force burst like a fury raiding the monasteries and settlements of Northumbria. For the settled, educated communities who suffered the first attacks the impact was fearsome These wild Norse men plundered, robbed, raped and murdered. They desecrated the holy shrines. We have such graphic descriptions of their impact as the communities they attacked were the recorders and keepers of Anglo-Saxon history.

That the Vikings were motivated by very similar forces that had caused the Anglo-Saxons to raid and then settle 300 years before the Vikings, did not seem to dawn on Anglo-Saxon England. Then, after the first raids on the Lindisfarne monastry, the Vikings turned northwards to attack the Scottish Isles and southwards to attack Northern France. Suddenly again in 835 with no prior notice or reason the wild men, the Danes or Norse men as the Anglo-Saxon historical chroniclers called the Vikings, attacked Northumbria. Raid was followed by raid, then years of settlement by Viking communities or tribes. For thirty years the people of Northumbria, Mercia and East Anglia knew few summers without some Viking incursions, settlement or payment of ransoms for the raiders to leave communities in peace.

## Alfred - Great for Many Reasons

Alfred of Wessex has long been held up as a great king. His reputation comes from his dogged resistance to the Viking invasions of his country, his great love of justice, the arts and books. Faced with overwhelming defeat at the hands of a huge Viking invasion army in 876, he retreated to the wetlands of Somerset and from there conducted a guerrilla warfare campaign against the Danish invaders. He broke out of his wetland base to win a victory over Guthrum at the battle of Eddington. Alfred forced the Viking king to accept a peace settlement that restricted the Danes to an area north of the Thames and the Wash. Further more he made Guthrum accept Christianity, by this move hoping to civilise the Vikings. With peace in his realm Alfred was able to reform his kingdom's legal system introducing many features that are still part of English law. Alfred established more monasteries as centres of book production than any other Anglo-Saxon ruler, as well as creating major works of art which are today regarded as the most outstanding items of Anglo-Saxon craftsmanship.

## Anglo-Saxons Against Vikings Again

Following Alfred's death a coalition of the Viking kings of Dublin and Northumbria brought hordes of Irish Vikings to settle in the north west of England. In 910 Alfred's son Edward the Elder beat these forces at the battle of Tettenhall in the present day Midlands. Then he and his son Athelstan employed a tactic of building fortified boroughs, slowly moving northwards their control of previously Viking held Danelaw. Athelstan sacked Viking York in 927, then in 937 at fierce battle at Bunanburgh, a site now lost to history, he totally wiped out a Viking invasion force killing five Viking kings and seven earls. From this time the whole of the Viking northern England began to be ruled by a succession of Saxon lords with the Vikings paying allegiance and taxes to the Anglo-Saxon King Edgar, Athelstan's strong ruling son, who can be considered the first Anglo-Saxon to hold sway over the whole of England. However this control was short lived for when the weak and ill counselled Ethelred the Unready came to the throne of England a message went out to the Viking world that England was weak again. Within two years Viking raids recommenced along the south coast and Irish Vikings again took over the north west of England. Throughout the 980's Viking summer raids became the norm for Anglo-Saxon England again. Ethelred the Unready's tactic was to try to get local forces to resist the fierce Viking onslaught and then when that failed pay off the invaders with ever growing amounts of 'Danegeld'. So in 991, Olaf Tryggvason attacked the Thames estuary with a force of ninety three warships. The local thane resisted this latest Viking attack so valiantly that he

# Background Information for Class Lessons

was celebrated in the Anglo-Saxon famous poem called the Battle of Maldon, Ethelred paying off the Vikings after their battle triumph with twenty two thousand pounds of gold and silver. They returned to their Scandinavian homelands and used their Danegeld to raise an even bigger fleet for the next summer's invasion. The year 991 saw Svein Forkbeard with 94 Viking ships beaten off from London by local forces, then they raided Anglo-Saxon towns along the south coast. Ethelred pacified them this time by agreeing to them over wintering in Southampton and paying them eighteen thousand pounds for a peaceful winter. This pattern of large organised Viking attacks on Anglo-Saxon towns continued with ever larger payoffs from the weakly led Anglo-Saxons. By 1002 the price of the payoff for peace was £24,000; by 1007 it was £36,000; 1010 saw Olaf the Fat pull London Bridge down, immortalised in the nursery rhyme ; 1011 saw a £48,000 ransom paid by the Anglo-Saxons of Kent for their Archbishop of Canterbury only for the Viking raiders to kill him in a drunken orgy.

## Knut Takes Over Anglo-Saxon England

In 1013 an eighteen year old Viking, Knut, raided England with his father Svein Forkbeard at the head of an enormous fleet. Northumbria was taken. Then the Vikings were repulsed from London, moving to the Wessex coast. Their fierce raiding led to the surrender of that area. Mercia was attacked and the Anglo-Saxon forces there surrendered to Svein Forkbeard. The victorious Vikings returned to attack London again this time more successfully as Ethelred the Uready had fled with his family to Normandy. Svein was now the virtual king of all England, and the Saxons were forced to swear allegiance to him. Svein's rule was short however as he died in 1014 in Wessex. The young Knut retreated with his Viking forces to their Danish homeland, Ethelred returned from Normandy and it looked like the Anglo-Saxons would rule again. However Knut returned in 1016, this time with a force of 200 ships, but as his Viking force sailed up the River Thames for a showdown with Ethelred the Unready, the Saxon king died. London submitted, and Knut was proclaimed King by the defeated London Anglo-Saxons. Edmund Ironside rallied the Anglo-Saxon forces and led a series of inconclusive raids against Knut's forces only for Edmund to die in 1016 before he could defeat the Danish invaders. On 30th November 1016 all England had its first Danish Viking king, Knut. He brought twenty years of much needed peace to England. He sought to stabilise the country, placating the Anglo-Saxons in his lands by reissuing old laws, emphasising impartiality to both Viking and Saxons alike, ensuring proper rights for all people in England. Threats from other Viking raiders were repulsed by mixed forces of Anglo-Saxons and Vikings and the land prospered. Knut's wise decision to support the Anglo-Saxon church as a powerful force for reconciliation helped heal years of strife between the two peoples. In 1019 Knut hurried to Denmark to be proclaimed king on the death of his brother. In 1028 he invaded Norway with a joint Viking/Anglo-Saxon force to drive Olaf the Stout from the throne of that country. For a few short years this civilised Viking, Knut, ruled a North Sea Empire that had long been the dream of the Viking raiders of England. Knut rebuilt the old Anglo-Saxon church at the heart of Wessex's old Anglo-Saxon capital, Winchester, in the strong Norman (continental Viking) style. It was here that Knut the Viking was buried in 1035 at the heart of the strongest Anglo-Saxon kingdom of Wessex.

## The Last Anglo-Saxon King of England

Ethelred's son, Edward the Confessor, a saintly, gentle man returned to rule England in 1035. England experienced a calm of sorts, but undercurrents and power struggles were emerging that would eventually disturb the succession in England on the death of the childless Edward. A Viking Dane, Godwin, had established himself in the old Anglo-Saxon lands of Wessex. He soon, by marriage and brutal take over, established his family as overlords of all of southern England. He married his daughter to Edward, seeking to control the Anglo-Saxon dynasty for his own family. From this base he and his argumentative sons Harold and Tostig sought to rule the whole country. The weak Edward allowed them to act in his name. Sibling rivalry saw Tostig build up a power base in the north amongst settlers of Viking origin, acquiring lands and allegiances throughout Mercia and Northumbria. Meanwhile Tostig's elder brother Harold consolidated his holdings in Wessex and Anglia, ruling the Anglo-Saxon kingdom from London, on behalf of a weak King Edward. With Edward sickly and approaching death, four factions plotted to seize power in a truly Anglo-Saxon family succession battle. Tostig, allied himself with Harald Hardrada, King of Norway, fresh from marauding Viking style raids on Russia. Tostig thought that a northern invasion would bring him support from his allies in his strongholds of Mercia and Northumbria. Harold Godwinson thought that he would command the situation from his power base close to the centre of the kingdom in London.

The Viking descendent William, Duke of Normandy claimed the throne through his inherited links with Edward the Confessor's family. On Edward's death the power struggle was set in motion. Harold Godwinson had himself crowned King in London. Harald Hardrada and Tostig invaded, marching on York in true Viking raider style. William prepared his fleet of Viking style boats and awaited favourable winds for his invasion. Harold Godwinson, in traditional Anglo-Saxon manner, rushed to meet the invading threat. He won a famous victory at Stamford Bridge, killing Tostig and Harald Harada in the battle. He and his Anglo-Saxon house carls dashed south to confront the Norman invasion force outside Hastings. The Norman Vikings won the day. William was crowned first Norman King of England. He set about the destruction of any Anglo-Saxon resistance, laying waste huge tracts of land in the north and east of England and establishing a system of strategic castles to control his kingdom.

Norman knights took over Anglo-Saxon and Viking lands. The rule of the Anglo-Saxons in Britain was ended after six hundred years and their land, England, was controlled by a Norse French dynasty.

# Art Ideas on the Theme of Anglo-Saxons

## Ships and the Sea

The Anglo-Saxons came to Britain in a variety of ships and boats, which they had built with great care and skill. They often buried their chieftains or thanes in ships. Their rule over England was first weakened by Viking raiders in their long boats sailing across the seas to raid and settle, and finally conquered by the Normans whose army were transported across the channel in a variety of ships.

A class art project could start with the children's research into Anglo-Saxon boat and ship design. Their sketches from this research could then be used to make a class wall display with boats and ships in choppy seas battling with the waves and with the sea monsters which inhabit the folk tales of the Anglo-Saxons.

## Weapons and Warfare

Allow the children to research the shields of the Anglo-Saxons and their enemies the Vikings and Normans. This provides the theme for a class Anglo-Saxon weapons wall display with a selection of the shields coloured brightly in the reds, yellows, blues and greens of the originals. Let the children decorate black card cut out shapes of Saxon axe, spear and sword heads with the swirling interwoven patterns of Anglo-Saxon art in gold and silver. Add to this bronze or copper coloured Anglo-Saxon helmet shapes covered with the same patterns picked out this time in black, the completed display would be fit for an entrance hall display. Their research into the weaponry of the period could be channelled into the creation of a battle scene of Anglo-Saxon warriors fighting either their Viking or Norman counterparts

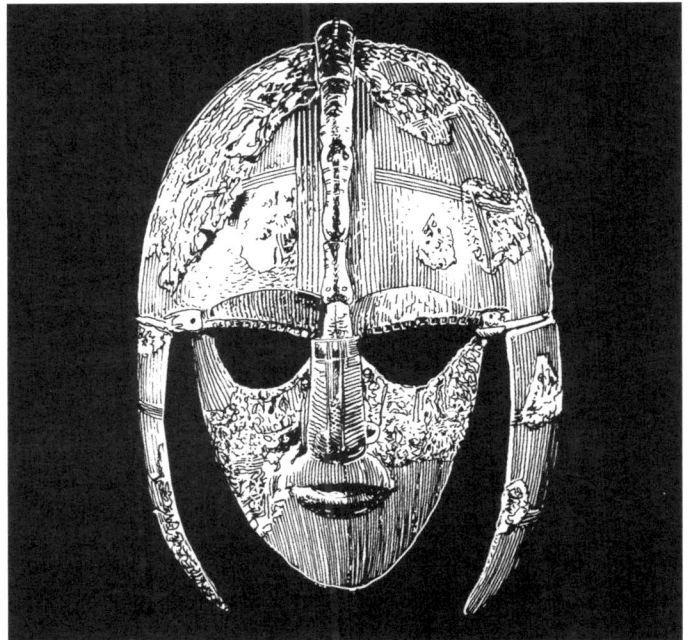

## Portraits

Head and shoulder portrait sketches of Anglo-Saxon kings, queens, warriors, monks, women, farmers, children, craftsmen and settlers will give children opportunities to practise their portrait drawing skills. A discussion of the moods and facial expressions of attackers, defenders, craftsmen, kings, queens, thanes and carls, or craftsmen and women, or settlers, could start from a study of part of an Anglo-Saxon folk tale, perhaps part of Beowulf, undertaken as a cross-curricular Literacy project. This could then be the inspiration for a wall display of the children's portraits accompanied by the children's character descriptions or their own versions of an Anglo-Saxon Folk poem or tale placed alongside their portraits.

# Art Ideas on the Theme of Anglo-Saxons

## Buildings

Although few truly Anglo-Saxon buildings survive intact, children can be shown the Anglo-Saxon influence in many of the old houses and cottages in many areas of England. Timber cruck framed houses with their wooden framed bays are direct descendants in a building time line of architecture.

Anglo-Saxon homes made from cardboard boxes and scrap materials could have stones, wood, reeds, straw or turf fixed onto wall or roof surfaces to copy the Anglo-Saxons use of the materials to hand in a variety of settlement sites.

Using individual children's models a class 3D Saxon village could be created. Add children's drawings of Anglo-Saxon houses as a backdrop and you will be providing practise in perspective and three dimensional drawing.

## Illuminated Manuscripts

The monasteries of later Anglo-Saxon England were power houses of a unique art style – the illuminated manuscript. The illuminated panels, frames and initial letters of the books created by the monks of the many monasteries provide excellent opportunities for art work. Children could be encouraged to provide an Anglo-Saxon frame for their best piece of written work showing the interwoven swirling patterns so beloved by the monks.

Encourage the children to produce their own initials as Anglo-Saxon bookplates. Picked out in gold, these would make a stunning display when backed by contrasting dark colours. A study of the methods of the monk's work would reveal their tools: the quill, the pestle, mortar and brush. Let children create their own Anglo-Saxon quill, and their own inks from crushed natural materials.

## Coins

The treasure troves of Anglo-Saxon England have thrown up a marvellous collection of gold and silver coins, whose lettering and images provide a superb collection of naïve folk art and craft work. The portraits of birds, animals and kings heads from these coins provide excellent observational drawing materials for children, which could then brighten up their topic work.

Using clay or plasticene the children create their own 3D coins, which could be painted gold, silver or bronze to make a super display. Create a class Anglo-Saxon treasure chest and have the children's coins spilling out from it to form the class's Anglo-Saxon coin hoard.

## Clothes

Provide the children with large cardboard cut outs of the human body, scraps of wool, linen, fur and leather materials. Then, from their own research, the children dress their person. Anglo-Saxon men and boys would wear a tunic as an upper garment reaching to their knees with breeches held close to their legs with criss-crossed leather bindings, a belt and a cloak fastened at the shoulder with a decorated pin would complete the outfit. Anglo-Saxon women and girls would have worn long linen or woollen dresses, over which would be a tunic fastened at the shoulder with a decorative pin brooch. A warm cloak and animal skin hat would complete an Anglo-Saxon female outfit. The class might like to improvise their own Anglo-Saxon clothes for an Anglo-Saxon Day. Children could make their own weaving frame from very stiff card. A shuttle made of similar card could then be wrapped with scrap wool and the children could weave their own pieces of Anglo-Saxon material.

## Jewellery

Anglo-Saxon men, women and children all wore jewellery and many fine examples have been found in archaeological digs throughout England. Brooches worn on shawls, tunics and cloaks were popular, the grander the brooch the more important the person. Provide the children with card cut into brooch shapes, coloured paper or foil and gold, silver and bronze crayons and they will make a wealth of Anglo-Saxon brooches. Safety pins could be fastened to the back. Necklaces and rings could be made from twisted string, the bright jewels which adorned the Anglo-Saxon originals could be created from crushed pieces of foil. All these could be worn by the children on an Anglo-Saxon clothes day.

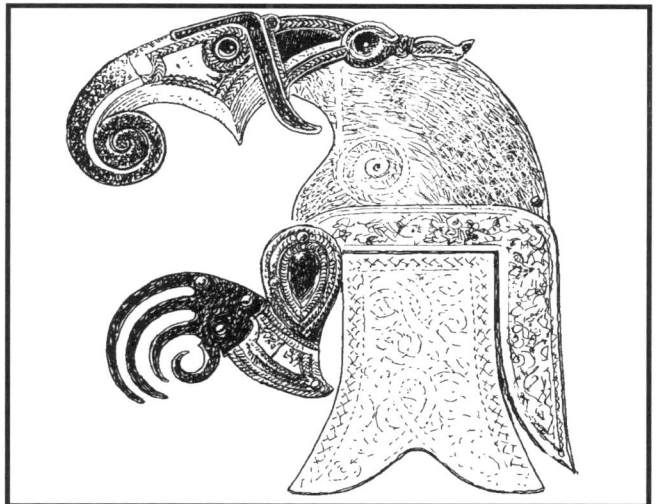

## Three Dimensional Art Work

Let the children research the jars, bowls, plates and utensils of the Anglo-Saxon period. Clay or plasticene could be used by the children to make slab bases. They could then use the coil method to build up their own 3D shape. The artefact will be made more authentic when the children smooth the outside with their fingers. Anglo-Saxon remains show brown, black, red and yellow glazes, which the children could replicate with paint and then varnish when dry. Alternatively, get the children to make sections of Anglo-Saxon 3D artefacts in clay or plasticene. Bury these fragments in a sand tray. Other pupils could then be given the task of providing labels for these 'finds', giving reasons for their use and name.

# Art Ideas on the Theme of Anglo-Saxons

## Art from Anglo-Saxon Poems and Stories

The Anglo-Saxons were great story tellers. Their tales in the chief's hall were made more fascinating by the beasts, sea creatures, demons, wild warriors and kings that populate the tales. A class study of sections of the Anglo-Saxon Beowolf poem, or the Battle of Maldon will provide inspirations for the children to produce a series of imaginative pictures, which could be used to form a class strip cartoon of the poems or stories. Allow the children to experiment with their monster designs in a range of collage materials to produce a class wall display of the fierce beasts from the stories of the Anglo-Saxons.

## Anglo-Saxon Gods and Goddesses

The Anglo-Saxons represented their gods and goddesses as wild beasts. Their chief god was Woden, often represented on the top of warrior's helmets as a wild boar with mighty tusks. Alternatively, Woden, a master of disguise, was represented as a cunning intertwined snake found on Anglo-Saxon belt buckles. Woden was accompanied by his fierce Raven. Fierce billed ravens are to be found in early Anglo-Saxon artefacts. Thor, the mighty god of thunder, is shown with double spears or a mighty hammer. Frig, Woden's wife, was the goddess of fertility and growing things, who is often drawn on a cart filled with corn, pulled by mighty bulls or cows. After their research into this subject, encourage the children to make their own 3D models of the beasts used by the Anglo-Saxons to represent their gods. Use clay, plasticene, string or junk materials.

## Christian Anglo-Saxon Artefacts

The introduction of Christianity to Anglo-Saxon Northern England by the Celtic monks from Ireland via Iona brought the wonderfully intricate interwoven patterns characteristic of Celtic art to the Anglo-Saxons. Many of their churchyards or market places came to have large crosses in them with two sides covered in these interlaced patterns to show the immortality of Christ whilst the other two sides were separated into rectangular sections each with its carving of some part of the Bible story of Christ. Make a large 3D cross out of plywood, polystyrene, or junk materials. Paint it grey, then let different groups in your class reproduce the patterns and naïve scenes in relief work using clay, plasticene, plaster coated bandage, plaster and string, done as relief work and painted grey. Your class will have produced a lasting piece of art work for a school entrance hall.

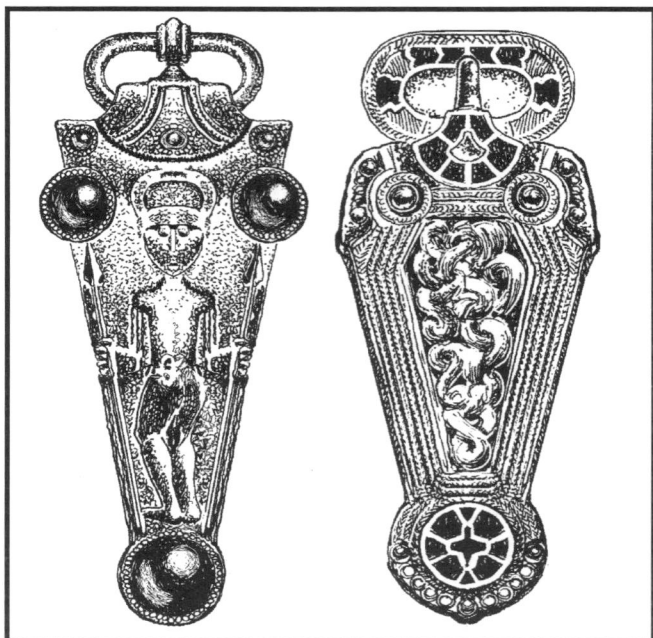

# Anglo-Saxons in Britain Timeline

## Task A:

Cut out each Anglo-Saxon shield and paste it near to the correct place on the Anglo-Saxon Timeline on the next two pages. Some of the Anglo-Saxon shields do not have dates. You will have to research the dates from reference sources.

## Task B:

Add further dates and facts to your timeline as you study the Anglo-Saxon era.

Offa becomes King of Mercia

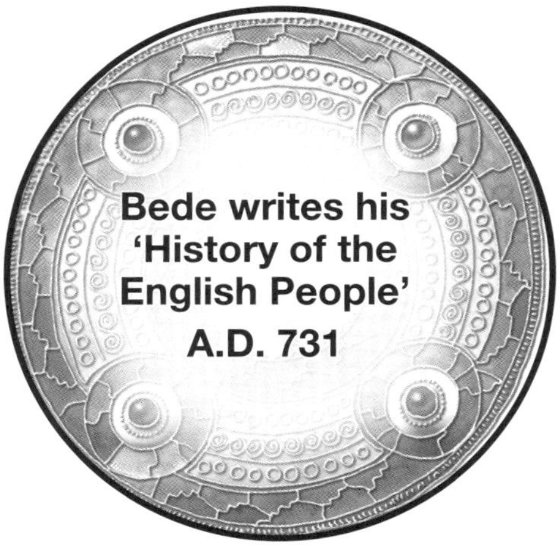

Bede writes his 'History of the English People' A.D. 731

Knut, a Viking King of England 1016

Viking raiders attack Lindisfarne Northumbria A.D. 793

Augustine sent from Rome to convert Anglo-Saxons to Christianity.

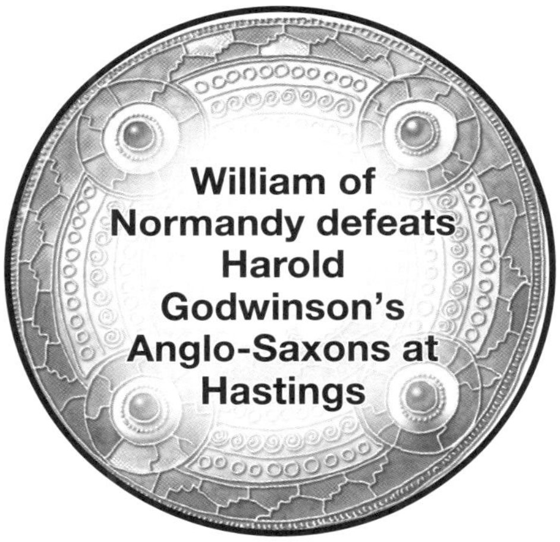

William of Normandy defeats Harold Godwinson's Anglo-Saxons at Hastings

Circa A.D. 625 A King is buried at Sutton Hoo.

The Battle of Maldon 991, celebrated in Saxon poetry

Alfred King of Wessex defeats Guthrum's Danish Vikings at Eddington A.D. 878.

Around 450 A.D.
Anglo-Saxon
Hengist and Horsa
land in Britain.

| A.D. 400 | A.D. 450 | A.D. 500 | A.D. 550 | A.D. 600 | A.D. 650 | A.D. 700 |

# Britain Timeline

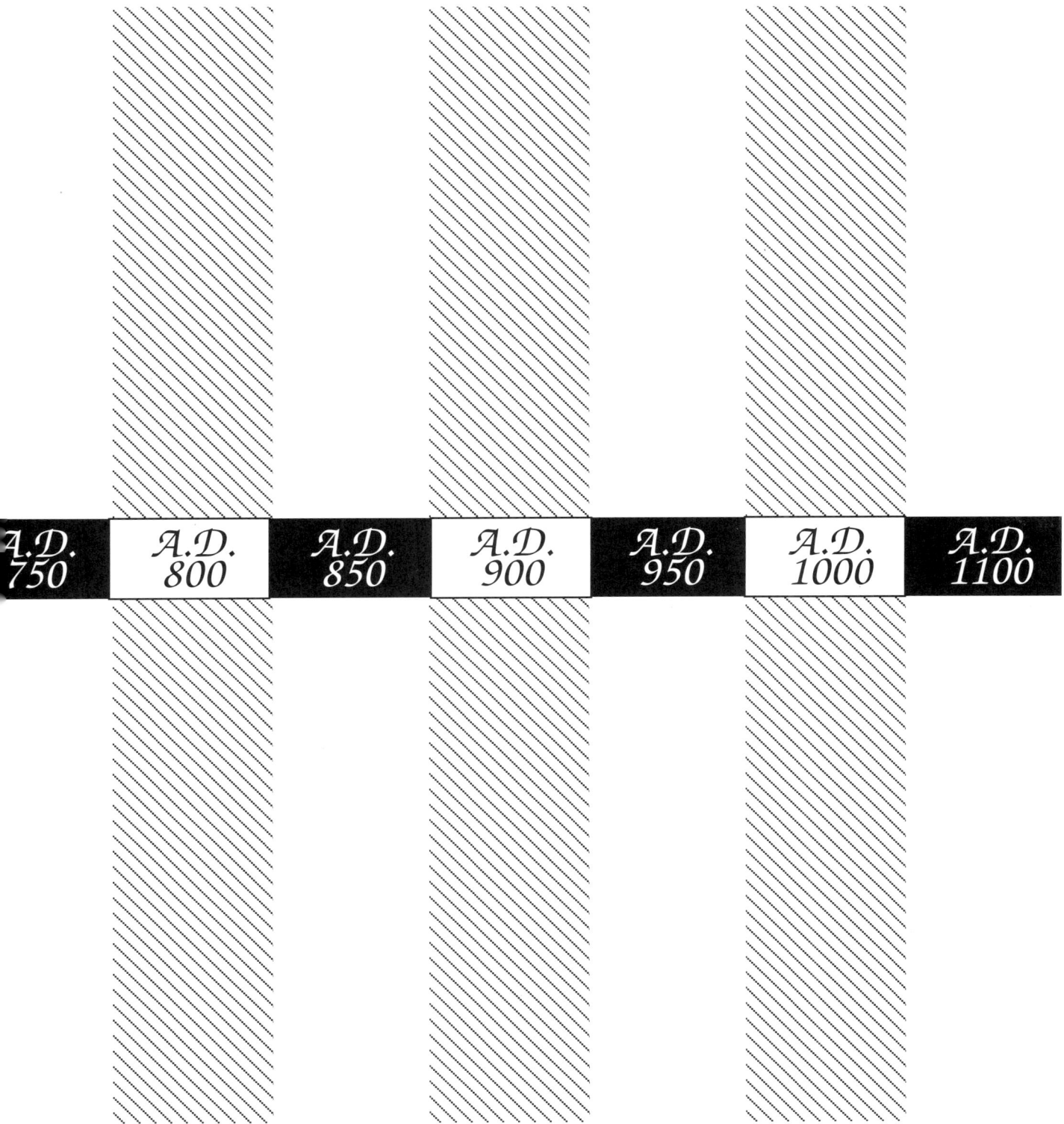

A.D. 750 | A.D. 800 | A.D. 850 | A.D. 900 | A.D. 950 | A.D. 1000 | A.D. 1100

# Different Views About an Anglo-Saxon Raid on Britain

**Egbert**
**The Saxon Chief**

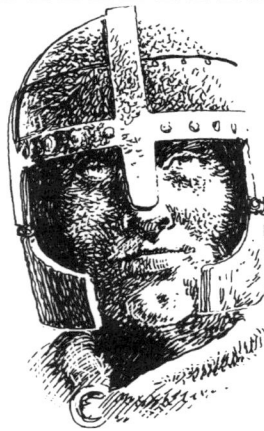

**Marcus**
**The Roman British Leader**

**Llyn**
**The Celtic Servant**

## Task A : Understanding that there can be different views about the same event

Carefully read the statements below. Think about who might have made these comments choosing between Egbert the Saxon, Marcus the Roman Briton, or Llyn the Celtic servant. Cut out each statement and paste it under the correct character on your own sheet.

## Task B : Describing different views of the same event

Imagine an Anglo-Saxon attack on a Roman fort on the shores of Britain. Write a Roman Briton soldier's view of the battle and then write a Saxon's view of the same attack.

I don't think that we have enough fighters to push the sea raiders back into the sea.

My men have heard that there are many rich things to grab, left by the Romans in Britain.

I am frightened that I will have my house burnt down by one side or the other in the fight.

If we win we may stay here as I think this island has good land for my people.

It is a shame that most of our best fighters have gone back to Rome to help the city.

My Roman master makes me fight the raiders when I just want to hide.

Both of these two sides just want to rule us poor Celts, they will use us as slaves.

Back in our Saxon lands there is not enough good farm land for all our people, that is why we came here.

Our great leader Agricola built our stone fort close to the shore so that we could stop any attack by ships.

We will sail in to the shore at night, so that we will surprise them in their fort by the shore.

My master has ordered me to bury all his gold and silver goods so that the raiders won't get them.

Our British people are not as good fighters as the legions used to be, they soon run from a fight.

Our women will love the fine gowns of the Roman ladies.

I will escape to the forest and hide from the fight.

All through our land there are stories of how weak the Romans are: they run back to Rome.

These men are wild. They live in wooden huts. They have no grand villas like ours.

Long ago my people were beaten by invaders, I think it will happen again.

Our God Thor will be with us in the fight.

# An Anglo-Saxon Raider's Kit

## Clothing

The Saxon raider wore a tunic made of wool. It was long and reached to his knees to keep him warm. He wore pants made of wool with leather straps tied round them to hold them tight. He wore leather shoes to protect his feet.

## Spear

......................................................

......................................................

......................................................

## Sword

......................................................

......................................................

......................................................

## Shield

......................................................

......................................................

......................................................

## Helmet

......................................................

......................................................

......................................................

......................................................

......................................................

### Task : Information Writing

Research in reference books, to help you find more information about the Anglo-Saxon Raider's Kit. The first one has been done for you. By each piece of kit write some sentences about what the kit is made from, what it was used for, and why you think it is important to the raider.

# How We Know the Anglo-Saxons Invaded Britain

## Task A : Interpreting Evidence

Carefully read Bede's words (a Monk writing in 731 A.D.) about how and when the Anglo-Saxons came to Britain, then cut each statement out and paste it on a separate sheet with the picture that matches the writing.

## Task B: Researching the Past

Research in reference books to find out all you can about the different Kingdoms of Anglo-Saxon England.

---

Hengist and Horsa, Saxon rulers, were invited by Vortigern to help him defend his lands in Britain.

In 449 A.D. Hengist and Horsa came in three longships, their plan was to rule Britain.

These invaders ruined the countryside and towns.

Buildings were burnt. Priests and people were killed.

A few people hid in the hills and forests.

They starved and had to give in to the invaders. They became slaves.

The Saxons became kings of all Britain.

More saxon invaders followed Hengist and Horsa. They sailed up rivers to attack rich towns.

✂

# Information from Anglo-Saxon Artefacts

**decorated horn drinking vessel**

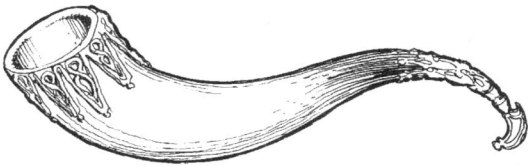

**spinning whorl**

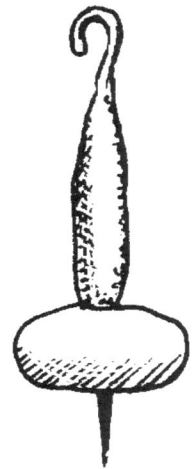

**trivet**

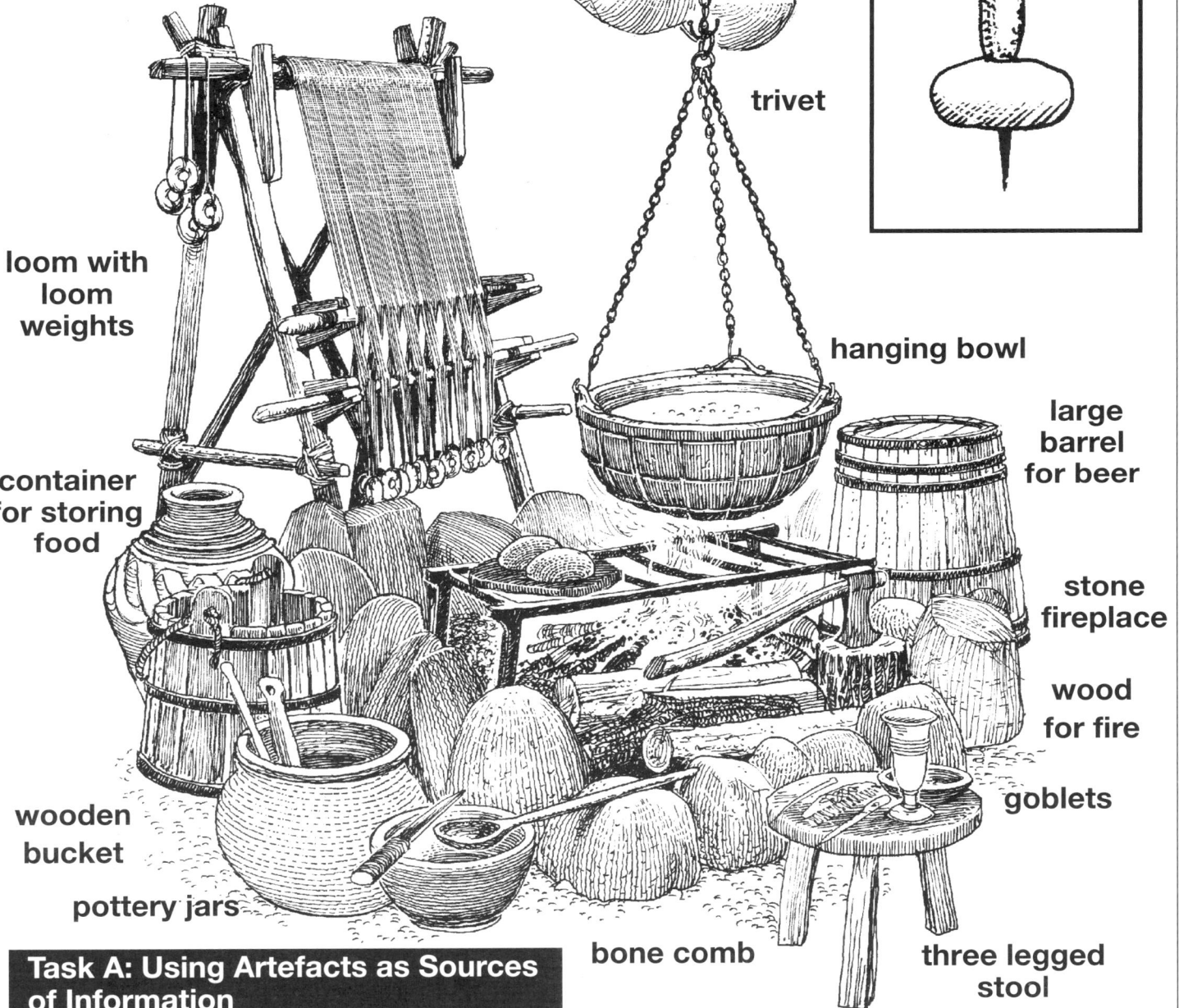

**loom with loom weights**

**hanging bowl**

**large barrel for beer**

**container for storing food**

**stone fireplace**

**wood for fire**

**goblets**

**wooden bucket**

**pottery jars**

**bone comb**

**three legged stool**

## Task A: Using Artefacts as Sources of Information

Study the picture of Anglo-Saxon artefacts.

List all the items that were used for cooking.

List all the items that were used for storing food or liquid.

List any article that could be used for drinking out of.

## Task B : Investigation

List all the utensils used in your own home for preparing, cooking and storing food. How are your meals are heated? Do you still use any kitchen items that are similar to those used by the Saxons more than 1500 years ago? If so name them?

# Everyday Life in an Anglo-Saxon Thane's Home

## The Thane's Hall

The thane was the head of a large family of people and their servants. The hall was one big room with low walls made of woven wood fences to mark out different living spaces. It would be dark as there were few windows. It was very smoky as the fire was in the middle of the hall, and there was only a small hole in the roof to let out the smoke.

## Work in the Hall

The women would spin wool into thread and then make cloth for clothes and blankets on a wooden loom. The men would make animal skins into clothes and shoes. They would sharpen and make tools and weapons in the hall.

## The Cooking Area

In the middle of the hall was a large patch of sand with a wall of stones around it. The fire would burn wood or peat. Women would cook on the fire using metal pots and pans. Around the fire would be storage jars made of pot to store food in. Hanging from the roof beams would be meat and fish. The smoke from the fire helped to keep the meat for a long time.

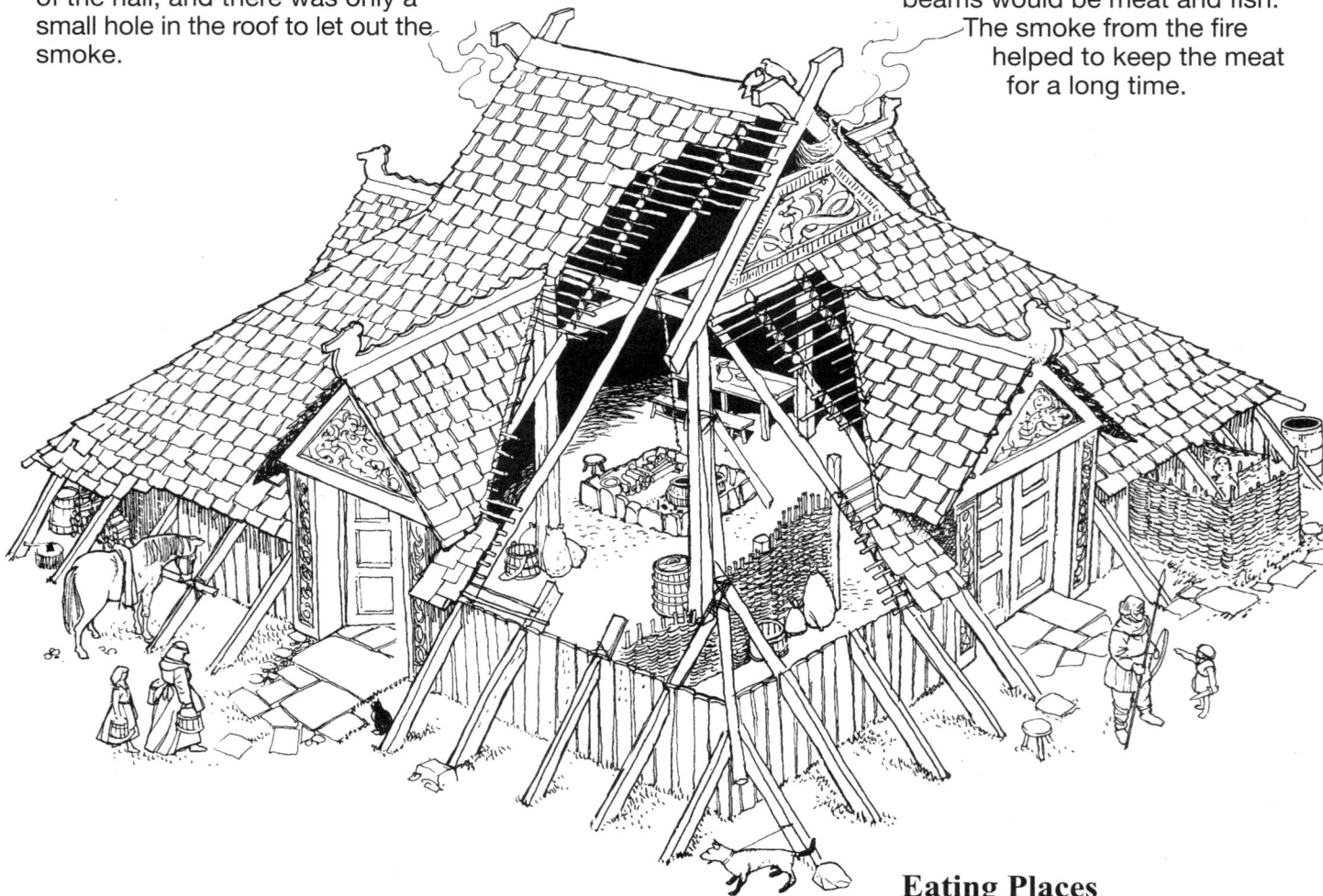

## Light in the Hall

Whale oil and animal fat were the fuel for the stone lamps which lit the hall. The fire would give light too. At feast times branches soaked in animal fat made torches which could be fitted into holders against the wall. It was not very bright in the hall at any time.

## The Toilet

Outside one end of the hall there would be a frame of branches around a wooden bucket. The bucket would have a lid with a hole in it. This was the toilet. It was emptied onto the land when it was full.

## Eating Places

Planks of wood were placed on trestles when the people wanted to eat. The thane and his close family would have a large table across the end of the hall. All the tables could be moved to make more space in the hall.

## Sleeping Places

The thane and his wife would have a large wooden bed with a mattress of straw and animal skins for their covers. Other people would sleep on platforms around the hall. They had the similar covers to the thane. The servants would sleep on the floor.

## Task A: Interpreting Evidence from Different Sources

After careful study of pages 18 and 19 choose which home you would have preferred to live in in Anglo-Saxon times in England. Give several reasons for your choice. Write your answers in full sentences.

# Everyday Life in a Poor Anglo-Saxon Home

## The House

The house was small, with just one room. It had a frame made from wood. The gaps in the frame were filled with tree branches. These were covered in mud, which was then covered with lime. The roof was made of a thatch of reeds.

## Toileting

The family would use a wooden bucket for their toilet. The bucket would be kept just outside the door of the house. When it was full the bucket would be emptied in the stream or on the land near the house.

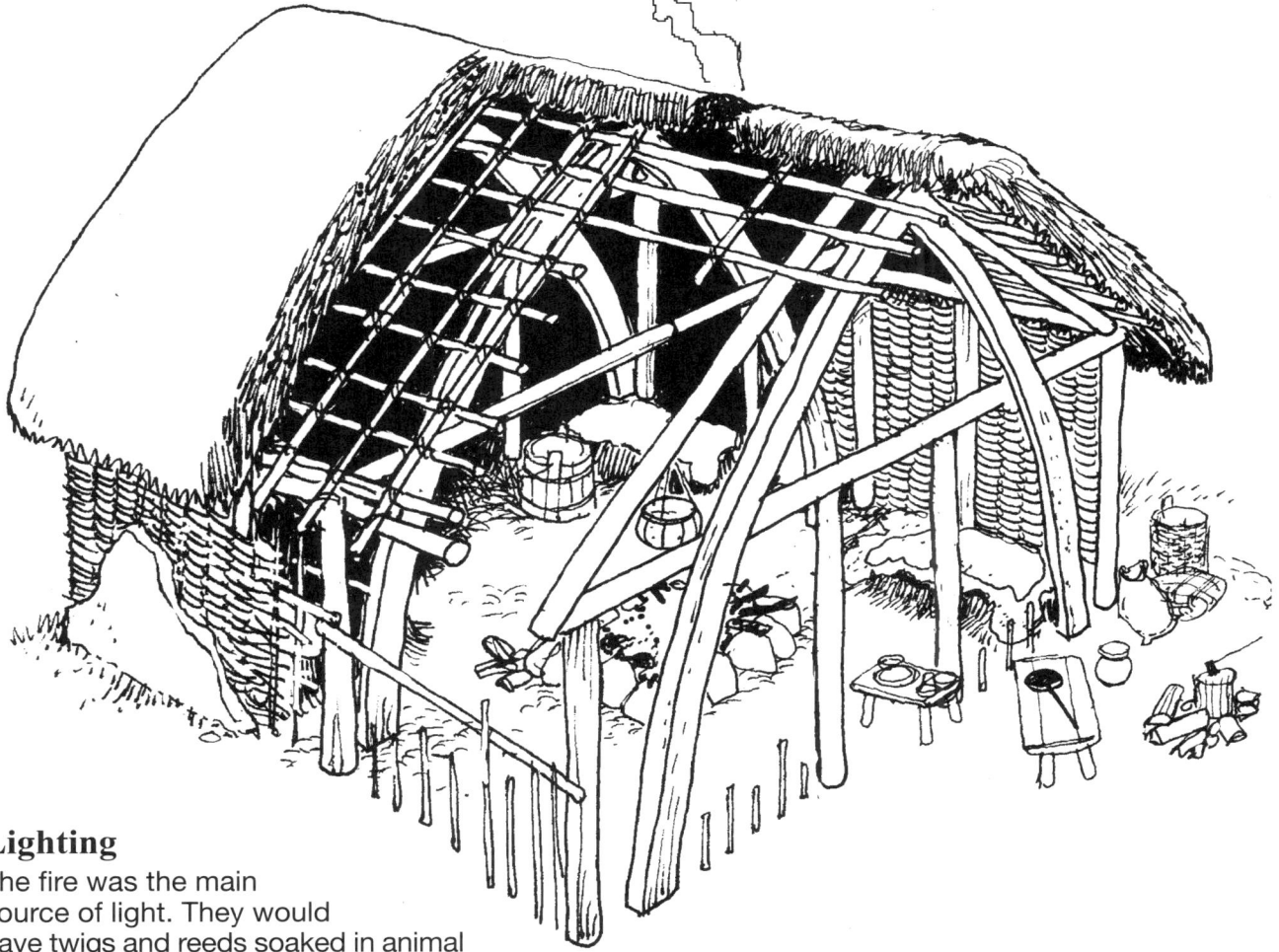

## Lighting

The fire was the main source of light. They would have twigs and reeds soaked in animal fat hanging from the roof for other lights.

## Washing

Most Anglo-Saxon houses were built near a stream or river. The women would wash the family's clothes on stones at the edge of the stream. The people rarely washed themselves, when they did they used the river or stream.

## Cooking and Heating

In the middle of the house was a square of stones. Inside this they made their fire. They cooked on the fire in a metal pan. The fire gave heat to the small house, but it also made the house smoky as there was only a small hole in the thatch to let out the smoke. Wooden barrels, pots, bowls and canvas sacks were used to store food in. Meat and fish would be hanging from the roof above the fire to keep it fit to eat.

## Furniture

They would have simple wooden benches and boards to use as seats. Their beds were raised platforms of earth covered with straw or reeds. They used animal skins to keep themselves warm.

## Task B : Using the Historical Evidence

Carefully study pages 18 and 19. Next, divide A4 paper into two down the middle. Put the label '**Good Points**' at the top of one column and the label '**Bad Points**' at the top of the other. List what you think are the good points and bad points about Anglo-Saxon homes in the columns you have made. Write in sentences and give the reasons for your choices.

# Be an Archaeologist and Solve the Mystery of the Sutton Hoo Site

An archaeological artist has drawn this picture to show us what the ship burial at Sutton Hoo might have looked like on the day the body was placed under the ship grave.

## Fact Box

Around 600 A.D. the Anglo-Saxons buried rich people in ships so that they could sail into a different world. They put their favourite objects in the grave, so that they could use them in the next world. They put a mound of earth on top of the ship to keep it safe.

## Task: Interpreting Evidence

Carefully study the goods placed in the Sutton Hoo ship. Why do you think those goods were put in the ship? Next, answer the questions below to solve the mystery of what sort of man was buried in the ship under the mound of earth. Give a reason for each of your answers.

Was the man under the ship a king? Yes or No ?

I Know this because ..............................................................................................................................

..............................................................................................................................................................

Was the man in the ship a Warrior? Yes or No ?

I know this because ..............................................................................................................................

..............................................................................................................................................................

Did the man in the ship like music? Yes or No ?

I know this because ..............................................................................................................................

..............................................................................................................................................................

Did the man in the picture like eating and drinking? Yes or No?

I know this because ..............................................................................................................................

..............................................................................................................................................................

# The Vikings Attack Anglo-Saxon England

In 866 Alfred, King of Wessex, hears the Vikings have raided East Anglia.

In 1069, William the Conqueror pays a Viking army to leave York and return to Denmark.

Ethelred the Unready pays Vikings to leave Wessex alone, 1012.

In 850 the Danish Viking army spends the winter in Thanet, raiding nearby towns.

Halfden, a Viking Lord, mints the first Viking coin in London in 871.

Harald Hardrada, Viking King of Norway, and his army are defeated by Harold Godwinson at the battle of Stamford Bridge, 1066.

A poem is written about the Battle of Maldon fought in Essex in 991, when an Anglo-Saxon army holds up a Viking raiding party.

In the summer of 786 three Viking ships raid the south coast of England.

Viking attack takes place at Lindisfarne in Northumbria. The church and monastery are destroyed in 793.

Alfred's Saxons defeat Guthrum's Danish Vikings at Chippenham 877.

By 899, The Viking Danes hold all of the East of England from the River Tees to The River Thames.

Knut, Viking king of Denmark, invades England with his Viking army, 1015.

## Task A:  Sequencing Historical Evidence

The facts about the Viking's attacks on Anglo-Saxon England above have been mixed up. Cut them out and paste them in the correct order on a fresh piece of paper.

# Anglo-Saxon Women's Lives
## Cooking, Baking and Farming

### Grinding the Grain

The women would grind the grain into flour for their bread using a stone quern with a wooden handle. They did this job every day.

### Baking and Cooking

In the middle of every house was a large fire. The women would cook meat, fish, soups and stews on the fire. Every day they baked bread on the fire. It was a long hot job.

### Kneading the Dough

The women kneaded the flour mixed with water in a long wooden trough. This made the dough. The women did this job every day.

### Making Butter and Cheese

The women would milk the family's goats, sheep and cows. They made the milk into butter by turning it in a churn for a long time. The women made cheese from milk which was a few days old.

### Helping on the Farm

The women helped cut the hay and harvest the grain in summer. They would put the meat from the sheep, goats, pigs and cattle in barrels full of salt to keep it from going bad. Sometimes they hung the meat over the fire to smoke. Smoked meat kept for a long time.

### Other Facts about Anglo-Saxon Women

A Saxon thane's wife might have slaves or servants to do her jobs. If the Anglo-Saxon men were away fighting then the women had to do all the work on the farm. The women had to teach the children how to do all the jobs on the farm and in the home. There were no schools.

# Anglo-Saxon Women's Lives
## Making Clothes

**Beating Flax:** After the flax plant had been cut, the women would put it in water for a week. Then they hit it on a board so that it was ready to spin.

**Carding Wool:** When the wool was cut from the sheep, the women would comb it straight with a metal comb. This got rid of knots or burrs in the wool.

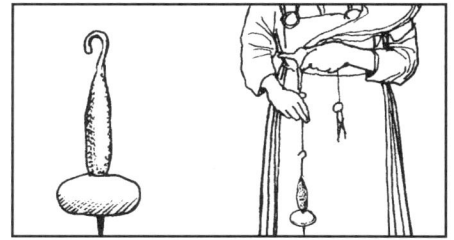

**Spinning:** Anglo-Saxon women would spin the wool on a spindle. This made the wool into thread. Then they could knit or weave the wool.

**Collecting Dyes:** The women would know which plants, or roots in the woods made different colours. They gathered them to make their wool different colours.

**Dyeing Yarn:** The women filled a big wooden bucket with hot water, put in the plants or roots they had collected, and put their wool in the water. They left it till the wool had changed to the colour they wanted.

**Weaving:** Many Anglo Saxon women had their own weaving loom. They made cloth on their loom. It was then made into clothes or blankets or sails.

## Task A: Comparing and contrasting evidence from the past

Carefully study pages 22 and 23. Then fill in the missing pairs of statements in the table below. The first one has been done for you.

## Task B: Interpreting evidence from different courses

Carefully study the two page about Anglo-Saxon women. Using this information, write a diary of a typical day in an Anglo-Saxon woman's life.

### Anglo-Saxon Women

1. Baked their bread on an open fire.
2. Cook their meals over an open fire.
3. Milked their cows by hand.
4. Made cheese from milk.
5. Wove their own cloth.
6. Make the cloth into clothes for the family.
7. Made butter from the cream of the milk.
8. Smoked their own meat and fish above the fire to keep them fresh.

### Women Today

1. Buy their bread from a supermarket
2. ................................................................
3. ................................................................
4. ................................................................
5. ................................................................
6. ................................................................
7. ................................................................
8. ................................................................

# The Story of Beowulf

## Task A: A Chronological Exercise

Beowulf is the Saxon's greatest poem. The Anglo-Saxon people would love to hear it recited at their feasts. The story is told in the boxes below. Read the story carefully as it has been muddled up. You need to cut out each box carefully and paste them in the correct order on another piece of A4 paper. Start your pasting with the box (1)

## Task B: A Cross-Curricular Exercise

Read the story of Beowulf that you have pasted together in the correct order again. Discuss the different characters in the poem and imagine the scenes from the poem. Now write your own script for a play about Beowulf's adventures that your class could perform for others

Beowulf heard about Grendel. He went to help Hrothgar fight Grendel. He tore Grendel's arm off, but Grendel escaped into the forest and died.

Hrothgar, king of the Danes had feasts at his hall which was called Heorot. The monster Grendel came to Heorot, the men were drunk or asleep. Grendel ate thirty of Hrothgar's men. He kept coming back to eat more men. Hrothgar did not know what to do.

Grendel's mother heard of her son's death. She came to Heorot to avenge her son. She took Hrothgar's best friend away to a haunted lake. Beowulf followed her, he found the head of Hrothgar's friend at the edge of the lake. Grendel's mother was hiding deep in the lake.

Beowulf took 12 men to fight the dragon. He fought the dragon alone. His shield did not stop the dragon's flames. His sword bounced off the dragon's skin. Most of Beowulf's men left him.

After his victory over Grendel's mother Beowulf went to his home. He became King and lived in peace. After many years a runaway slave hid in a burial mound where a fierce dragon lived. The slave stole some treasure from the mound and ran away with it. The dragon was angry and chased the slave. The dragon flew over Beowulf's hall at night. It blew fire at the hall and set fire to the crops and houses.

Beowulf went into the cave. Beowulf's sword Hrunting bounced off Grendel's mother's tough skin. She attacked Beowulf with a deadly knife. Beowulf grabbed a huge sword from the cave wall. He swung the mighty sword and cut off Grendel's mother's head. He had saved Hrothgar's people again.

# The Story of Beowulf

Only Wiglaf stayed to fight the dragon with Beowulf, the Dragon sank its teeth into Beowulf's neck. But Beowulf and Witlaf killed the dragon, then Beowulf died of his wounds. Witlaf buried Beowulf under a mound. Many Kings brought treasures to put in Beowulf's grave.

Someone gave Beowulf Hrunting, an old sword that had never been beaten. With Hrunting in his hand, Beowulf dived into the black waters of the lake. Many strange creatures tried to grab him. At the bottom of the lake there was a dry cave, Beowulf found Grendel's mother there.

✂

background

boat

fix spacers
between boat
and background

fix tabs to base

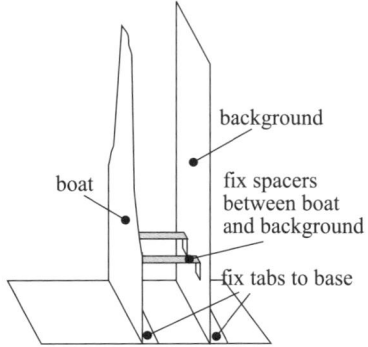

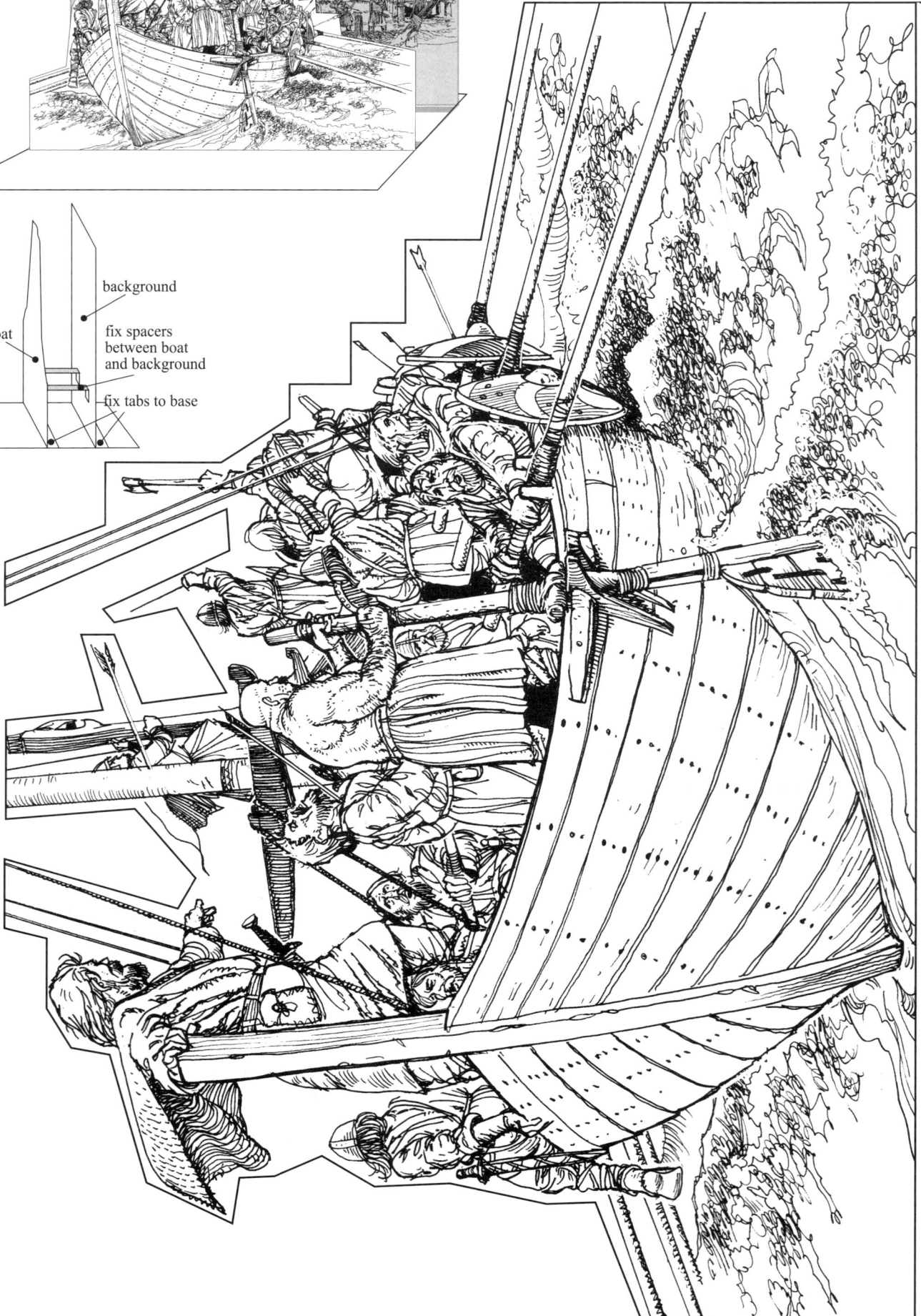

fix tab to base on page 28

# Raider's Pop Up Model

(1) Photocopy pages 26, 27 and 28 on to thin card. (2) Use reference books to help you write a short description of what is happening. (3) Colour the pictures appropriately. (4) Cut out the background, the boat, the base and the two spacers, following the black lines. (5) Assemble as shown in the small diagram on page 26.  ✂

## Anglo-Saxon Raiders Storm a Roman British Settlement

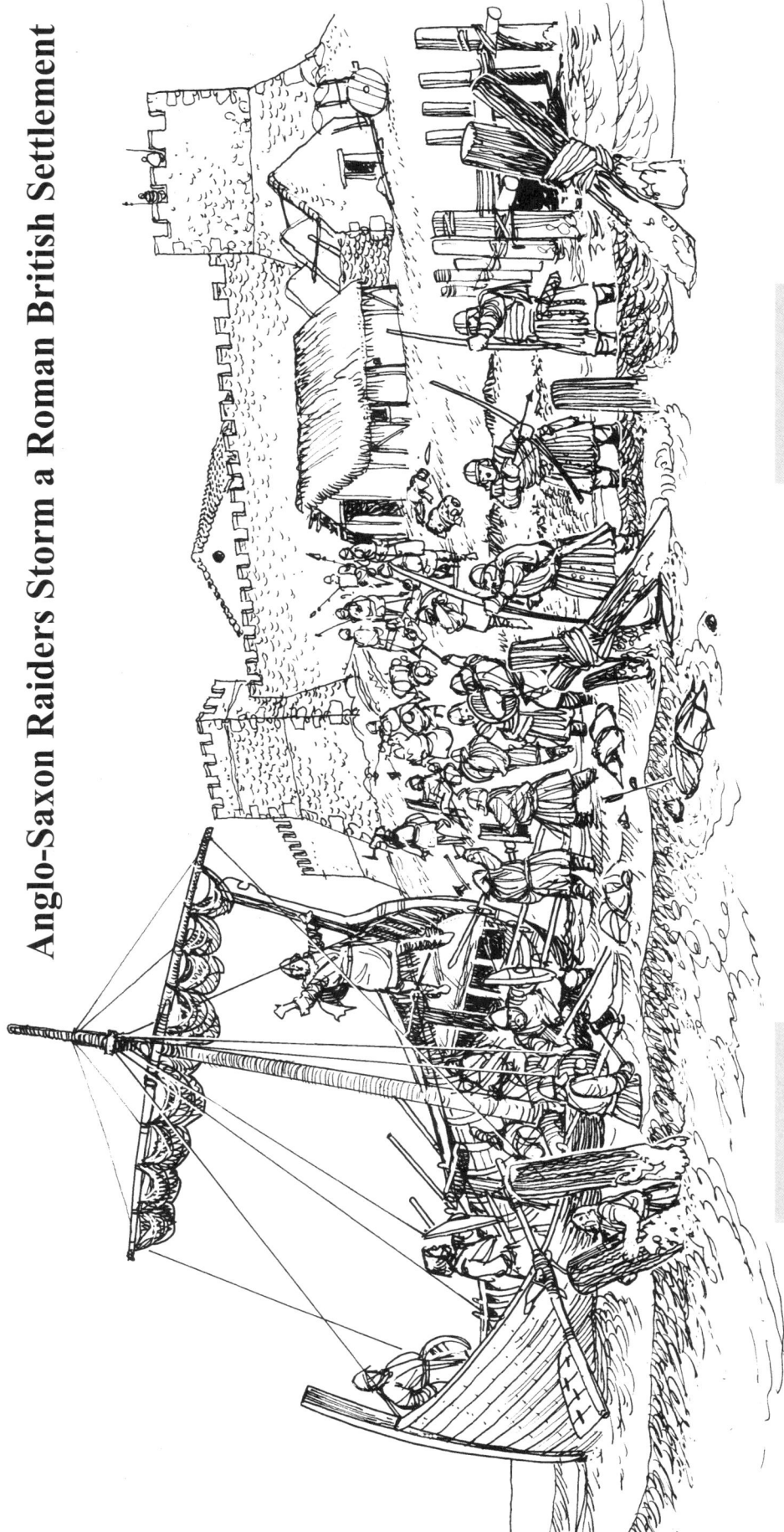

Stick one end of spacer here.

Stick one end of spacer here.

fix tab to base on page 28

Stick onto
background

spacer

Stick onto
cut-out boat

Stick onto
background

spacer

Stick onto
cut-out boat

Stick background on here

base

Stick cut out boat on here

# Crime and Punishment in Anglo-Saxon Britain

## Anglo-Saxon Laws

The kings in Anglo-Saxon times were expected to make the laws and punish those who did wrong. They had a group of friends or chief men of the kingdom to help them. This group of people called thanes, could make rules for their village or town. His court was called a moot or witan. There were no prisons as people who committed a crime were beaten or had their hands or feet cut off. Sometimes they were hanged.

## Oath Helpers

If the thane or king said you were guilty of a crime, and you went to the Witan or Moot to be tried, you could prove you were innocent if you could find enough people who would swear an oath on something holy and say that you had not done the evil deed. Anglo-Saxons believed if you told a lie as you swore the oath in the Witan or Moot your tongue would burst.

## Wergild

This was the money (gild) you had to pay if you wounded (wer) someone. Every Anglo-Saxon had a value in money. A Thane would be worth 1,200 shillings, if you killed a Thane you had to pay his family that price. If you could not pay you became their slave. A Churl, a poor man was only worth 100 shillings. Every part of the body had a price too. If you just wounded a person you had to pay for the part of their body you had wounded.

## Trial by Ordeal

If you could not find enough people to say you were innocent, you would face trial by ordeal. In trial by water, the person who had done the crime was tied up and thrown in a pond. If they floated they were guilty. If they sank they were innocent (but they might drown before they were pulled out). In trial by heat, the person accused had to carry a red-hot iron bar three paces without dropping it.

### Task

Form your own class witan or moot court. Choose a thane or king and their advisors. Next, make a list of imaginary Anglo-Saxon crimes. Draw lots for who in the class has to act as the criminals. Finally, hold a trial. Some people may want to be oath helpers. You will have to impose a punishment or wergild fine if the criminal is found guilty.

# The Anglo-Saxons Become Christians

### Irish Monks Come to Iona:

In 565 some Irish Christian monks sailed to Iona, a small island off the coast of Scotland. They set up a church there. Sometimes they travelled around to persuade the Scottish tribesmen to believe in Jesus.

### Oswald Invites Monks to Northumbria:

In 635 King Oswald of Northumbria invited some of the monks from Iona to come to his kingdom. Oswald was a Christian and he wanted the monks to preach to his people.

### The Monks on Lindisfarne:

The monks who came to Northumbria wanted a quiet place away from people where they could pray to God, so they went to live on the island of Lindisfarne in the North Sea.

### St. Cuthbert:

Cuthbert was a shepherd boy in Northumbria. He heard the monks from Lindisfarne teaching about Jesus. He grew up to be a great preacher. Cuthbert went to places and people who everybody else feared. He encouraged them to become Christians.

### Pope Gregory and St. Augustine:

Pope Gregory saw some fair haired slaves for sale in Rome. He found out they were from England. He decided to send St. Augustine to Kent to teach about Christianity.

### Christian Teaching:

King Ethelbert of Kent did not believe in the Christians teaching. He agreed to meet St. Augustine in the open air as he thought that the Christian's magic would not work there. But he loved the stories of Jesus and soon became a Christian.

### Monasteries:

By the end of the Anglo-Saxon rule in England there were hundreds of monks. They copied out stories from the Bible onto parchment. They drew beautiful patterns and pictures in their books. They prayed every day and night.

### Missionaries:

Once the Anglo-Saxons became Christians they spread the word of Jesus back to the countries they had come from in northern Europe. English monks like Boniface, Anselm and Lul became bishops in cities in Germany, Austria and Belgium.

## Task A: Using Evidence from Different Sources

Carefully read the text and study the pictures on this page. Carefully read each of the statements below, and from the evidence on this page decide whether each statement is 'true' or 'false' or, 'there is no evidence' for you to decide. Write a reason for your choice to go with each statement.

1. The monks who built the Church on the island of Iona came from Scotland.
2. King Oswald of Northumbria was killed in a battle against the pagan people.
3. The monks wanted to live on the island of Lindisfarne because they wanted to be quiet to worship God.
4. Cuthbert went to many places that other monks would not go near.
5. Pope Gregory wanted to go to England himself but he was too busy in Rome.
6. King Ethelbert was a bit afraid of St. Augustine's magic.
7. The monks did not pray so much because they were too busy writing books.
8. Many cities in Germany, Austria and Belgium had English bishops.

## Task B: Cross-Curricular Links

Research in reference books to write your own piece of Information writing about the lives of St. Cuthbert, and St. Augustine.

# The Anglo-Saxon Chronicles Campaign Game

## For up to 4 players

- Many different Anglo-Saxon tribes settled in Britain, each with their chieftain or thane in their own area of Britain.

- The tribes fought each other or made alliances or friendships with neighbouring tribes.

- At the same time as the Anglo-Saxons were invading from the east of Britain, the native Roman Britons or Celts were pushed further and further westwards until they were confined to the area of modern Wales and Cornwall.

- Eventually as a result of the tribal warfare there came to be 5 main Kingdoms: Kent, East Saxons, Wessex, Mercia and Northumbria.

- When the Saxons became Christians they built many monasteries to which they gave rich gifts. The monks and nuns in the monasteries produced many fine hand written books with beautiful pictures in them.

- Viking Raiders attacked the Saxon kingdoms and monasteries from about 793 A.D.

## Aim of the Game

You are a wandering Anglo-Saxon in Saxon England, seeking your fame as a warrior in as many conflicts as you can.

On your way you rest at some of the many monasteries.

You gather treasures as you go as trophies of your courage in battle or your devotion to God.

## How to Play the Game

1. Your teacher sets the time limit for your game.

2. Each player throws the die once. The person with the highest score chooses his Saxon Warrior first, shakes the dice and moves that number of places from the Start at Winchester in the direction of the arrows.

3. If the player lands on one of the rectangles they collect one one of the spears, shields or crosses from the correct treasure box.

4. The winner is the person who returns to the start with most crosses, spears, or shields.

## You Will Need:

- A die
- A shaker
- The map on page 32 and 33 each enlarged to A2 and pasted on thick card.
- A Saxon Warrior piece for each player.
- A supply of crosses, shields and spears in each treasure box. You will need to photo copy lots of these.

### Saxon Warrior pieces

*Cut out the warriors and fold them so that they end up like this. If you want you can cut away the surplus black area.*

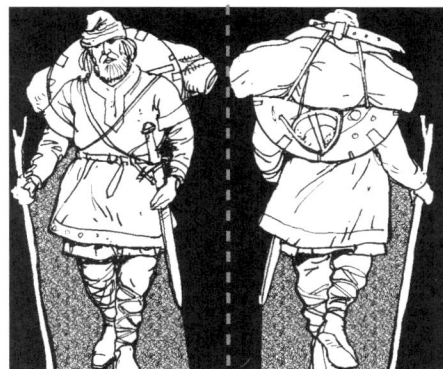

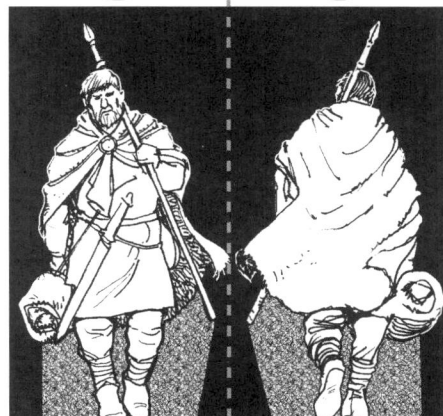

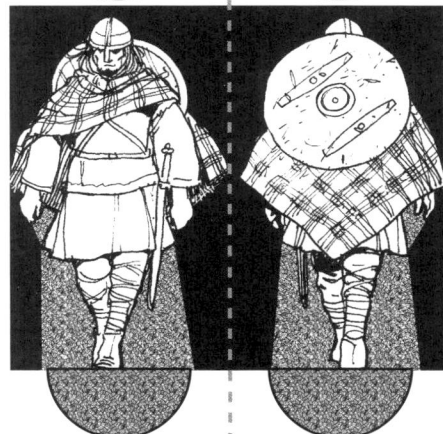

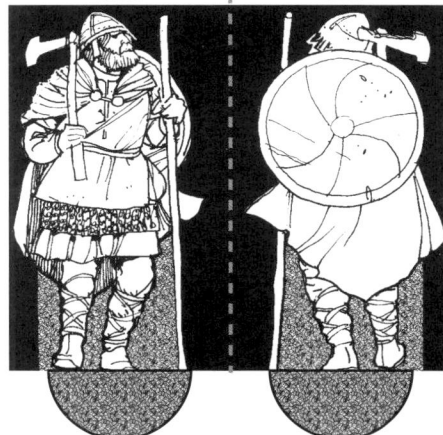

| shield | spear | cross |
|--------|-------|-------|
| 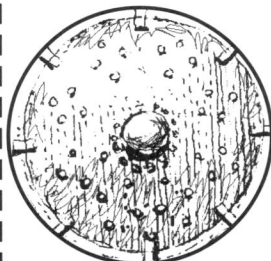 |  |  |

# Serpent Spear Chest

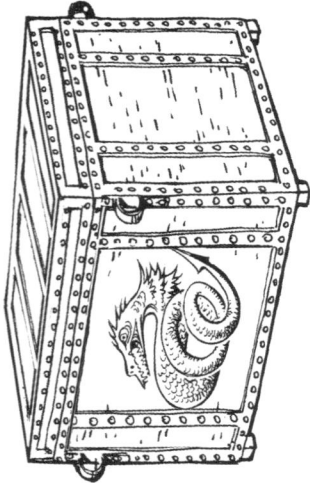

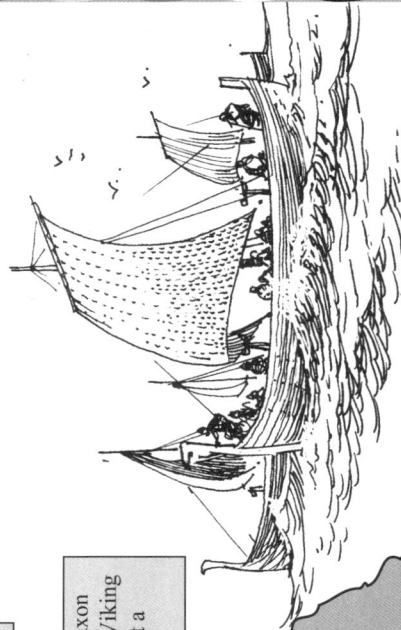

**8** Visit St. Cuthbert at Lindisfarne. You gain a cross.

**9** Bede shows you Saxon Chronicle. Collect a cross.

**10** Defend a Saxon town from Viking raid. Collect a shield.

**11** Slay King of Norway at Battle of Stamford Bridge. Gain a spear.

**12** Help build wall around a Saxon town. Collect a shield.

**6** Battle against Irish Viking Raiders. Collect a spear.

**5** Set up new monastery. A monk gives you a cross.

**4** Fight border battle against Celt attack. Collect a spear.

**7** Raid a Celt camp. You gain a spear.

NORTHUMBRIA

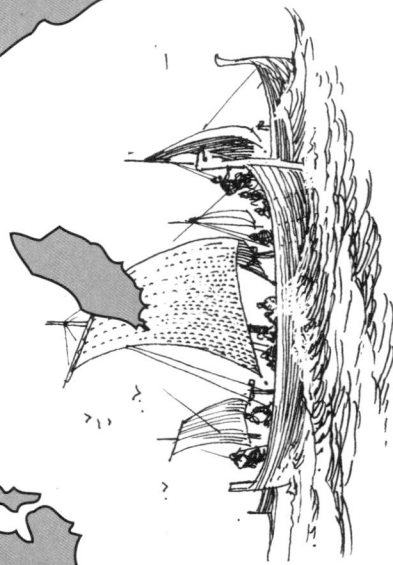

EAST SAXONS

You gain a shield.

**15** You fight to defend London from Viking attack. You gain a spear.

KENT

**16** You take part in the Battle at Hastings. For your bravery you gain a spear.

A war between the Saxon Tribes. You gain a spear

WESSEX

**17** You attend Alfred's School for priests. You gain a cross.

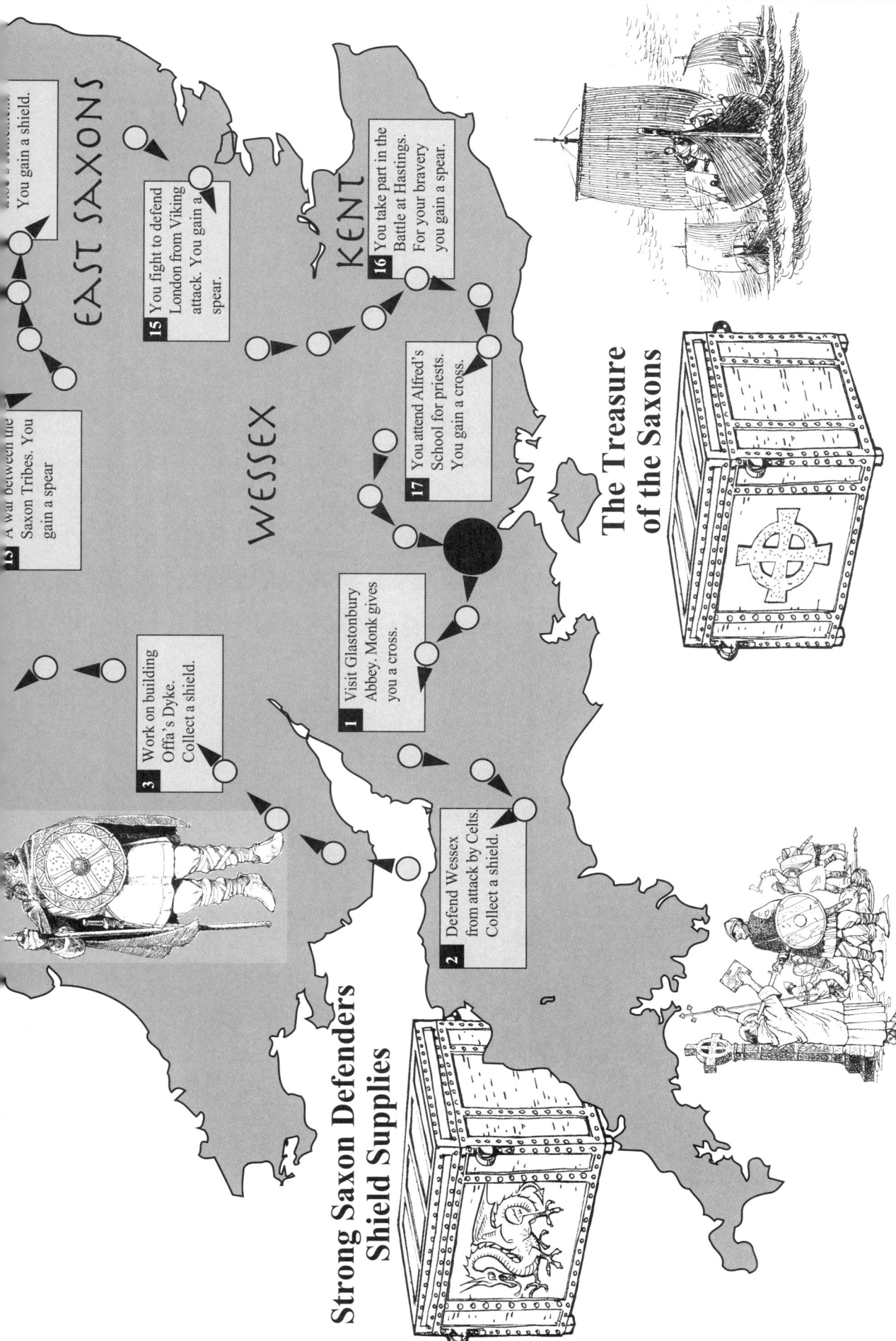

**The Treasure of the Saxons**

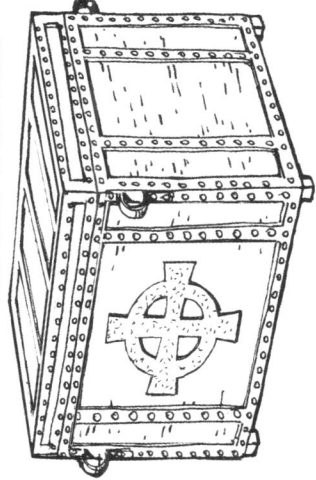

**3** Work on building Offa's Dyke. Collect a shield.

**1** Visit Glastonbury Abbey. Monk gives you a cross.

**Strong Saxon Defenders Shield Supplies**

**2** Defend Wessex from attack by Celts. Collect a shield.

THE ANGLO-SAXON CHRONICLES CAMPAIGN GAME

# Anglo-Saxon Runes and Riddles

## Runes and Rune Stones

Archaeologists have found many pieces of stone, bones, antlers, rings, brooches, pottery and skin from the time of the early Anglo-Saxon settlers in England with strange markings on them. Clever researchers have found that these markings were letters in a form of writing the Anglo-Saxons used before monks from Ireland and Rome taught them writing like our own. The Anglo-Saxons called these markings runes. They believed that the runes had magical powers. Leather bags with lots of stones each with a separate rune carved on them have been found. Researchers believe that these rune stones were used by the Anglo-Saxons to tell their future. A person would pick out 3 rune stones from the bag and a wise man would tell their future from the meaning of the runes. The first stone they chose stood for their present life, the second stood for the problem the person might face in the future and the third stone stood for the solution to their problem.

## An Anglo-Saxon Rune Stone Alphabet

The Anglo-Saxons also used the runes as an alphabet to send messages. Archaeologists have put together an alphabet for us to use. You can see a copy below.

You will see that some of our letters have not got a rune symbol to stand for them. You will have to design your own rune symbol for those modern letters.

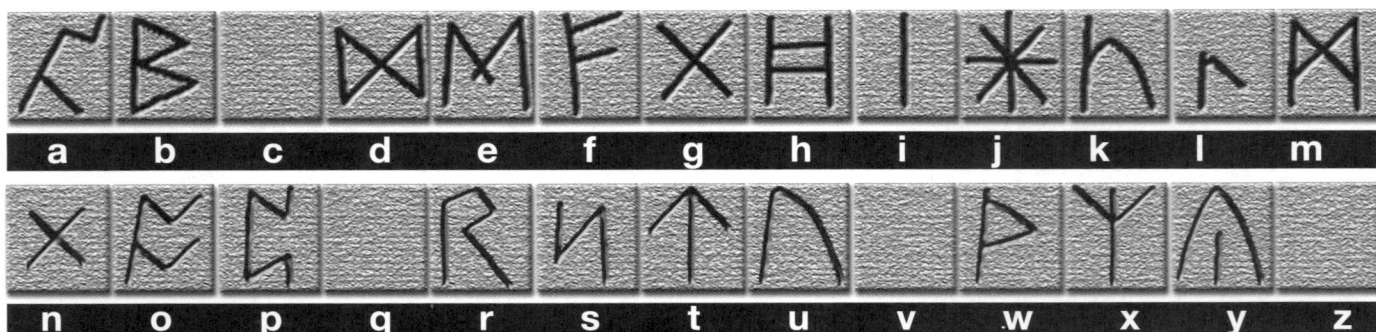

| a | b | c | d | e | f | g | h | i | j | k | l | m |
|---|---|---|---|---|---|---|---|---|---|---|---|---|

| n | o | p | q | r | s | t | u | v | w | x | y | z |
|---|---|---|---|---|---|---|---|---|---|---|---|---|

## Task A: Using different historical sources

Write your full name in the Anglo-Saxon rune alphabet, then write a message for your friend to translate into modern English.

**Your Name in Rune Alphabet:**

......................................................................

......................................................................

**Your Message in Rune Alphabet:**

......................................................................

......................................................................

**Your Friend's translation in modern English:**

......................................................................

......................................................................

## Task B: Anglo-Saxon Riddles

The Anglo-Saxons loved to make up riddle poems for their friends to solve. The poems gave clues as to what an everyday object was and the listeners had to guess what object was in the riddle.

In the boxes below are four Anglo-Saxon riddles for you to solve. Draw the object in the blank box next to the riddle, and label the object.

| | |
|---|---|
| I hang from your belt<br>Below your tunic<br>Take me out<br>I fit in a hole<br>I open a treasure | |
| I come from a cow<br>I'm curved and round<br>I can make a loud sound<br>I can be filled<br>You can drink from me | |

| | |
|---|---|
| I keep you dry<br>I touch the sky<br>I may be straw<br>I may be stone<br>Birds rest on me | |
| I have three legs<br>On my bottom a bottom can rest<br>I love to be near a table<br>Whenever I am able | |

## Task C: Cross-Curricular Links

Try to make up some riddles of your own for your friends to solve.

# Make An Anglo-Saxon Magazine

On this page you have two news reports and two pictures from your illustrators. Complete the next two pages ready for your magazine's printing. Cut these out and paste them under your sub-editors suggested titles. Notice that there are some story lines and pictures missing. As print day is tomorrow you will have to research, draw and write these items yourself to fill the empty column space. All the subtitles you need have been provided for you.

*Our Artist's drawing of Bede at work writing his book about 'The History of the Anglo-Saxons' at the monastery of Jarrow in 731.*

*Norman Duke William extracts promise from his Saxon Prince Hostage.*

Harold Godwinson prince of Wessex had sailed to Normandy, but his ship was swept off course and he was captured by the Lord of Brittany. Duke William of Normandy paid a ransom to set Harold free. He then tricked Harold into swearing an oath that Duke William of Normandy would be next King of England after Edward the Confessor's death. Harold is said to be sailing home to England soon, and now says he is the rightful heir to the English Crown. Watch out for a quarrel and maybe a battle between the two men when Edward the Confessor dies.

*A Ships Burial for an Anglo-Saxon Thane at Sutton Hoo.*

*Our Artist's impression of the baptism of the Viking Danish leader Guthram after his defeat by Alfred of Wessex at the battle of Chippenham in 878.*

On a cold and windy day, a great warrior thane was laid to rest with his famous ship. All his people followed in a sad procession behind his body as he was buried under the ship, with his helmet, shield , sword and many of his brooches and other jewellery. It is thought that the ship was positioned facing the sea, from where the thane had sailed into England to set up a settlement for his people. The ship had been laid in a pit, and then, as is the custom of his people, the ship was covered with a high mound of earth.

# ANGLO-SAXON TIMES

AVAILABLE MONTHLY          PRICE TWO PENNIES

## Norman Duke Extracts a Promise from his Anglo-Saxon Captive.

## Jarrow Monk Bede Writes the Story of the Anglo-Saxons in England.

*Our Artist's drawing of Bede at work writing his book about 'The History of the Anglo-Saxons' at the monastery of Jarrow in 731.*

..................................
..................................
..................................
..................................
..................................
..................................

## Anglo-Saxon Raiders Terrify South Coast Roman Britain Fort

..................................
..................................
..................................
..................................

## Offa, King of Mercia, Builds Huge Barrier to Keep Out the Celtic Britons

..................................
..................................
..................................
..................................
..................................
..................................
..................................
..................................
..................................
..................................

# ANGLO-SAXON TIMES

AVAILABLE MONTHLY      PRICE TWO PENNIES

**King Alfred of Wessex makes Danish
Viking Leader a Christian After
Battle of Chippenham**

...............................................................

...............................................................

...............................................................

...............................................................

*Our Artist's impression of the baptism of the Viking
Danish leader Guthram after his defeat by Alfred of
Wessex at the battle of Chippenham in 878.*

## A Great Poem Celebrates the Fierce Battle of Maldon
## Between a Battling Anglo-Saxon Thane and the Danish Raiders

.......................................................................................

...............................................................

...............................................................

...............................................................

...............................................................

...............................................................

...............................................................

## A Ships Burial for an
## Anglo-Saxon Thane at Sutton Hoo

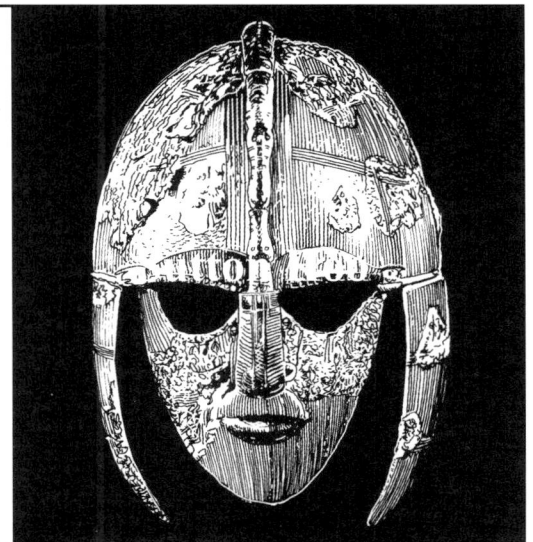

# Make your own Anglo-Saxon Illuminated Letter

At the end of Saxon Times there were more than 300 monasteries in England. One of the jobs the monks did was to make hand written books. The monks drew very fancy letters to start each page in these books.

## Task A:

Above is a kit of pieces from which you can build your own initial. You may need to use more than one of each piece. Study the small examples to give you some ideas.

## Task B:

Research in reference books to find other examples of Saxon illuminated letters. Make copies of them for a classroom display of the Saxon Monks' work.

# Farming in Anglo-Saxon England

## Task A: Using information from a range of primary sources.

On this page are four drawings from an Anglo-Saxon calendar of the farming year, and four pieces of writing from different Anglo-Saxon books. They have become separated. Cut each picture and piece of writing out carefully and paste them onto a piece of A4 paper so that they tell the story of a year in Anglo-Saxon farming. Start with the spring picture and writing.

## Task B: Showing empathy for events from the past.

Imagine you are the Lord of an Anglo-Saxon village. Write an account of the orders you would give your people for their farm work in one year.

"My Lord orders all our people to work in the harvest. It is hot work in the high sun of summer. We stop often to sharpen our scythes. Some men fork the cut hay into piles. The women tie the piles into stooks to dry the grain".

"With the fall of leaves and before the winter sets in, our Lord commands all men of the village to the winnowing circle with our flails. We beat the stalks to gather the grain from the ears of corn. Others carry away the grain to dry barns, to store it for our daily bread."

"I work hard. I go out at daybreak, driving the oxen to the fields, where I yoke them to the plough. However cold the winter is, I dare not stay at home for fear of my Lord. Every day I must plough an acre or more. I have a boy driving the oxen with a goad. He is hoarse with shouting in the cold."

"With the first warmth of spring I go out onto the fields to scatter the seed, I pray for rain to follow so the seed will start to grow. A boy comes after me and spends many long days in the field with a rattle to scare the birds off the seed."

## Anglo-Saxon Words Give U

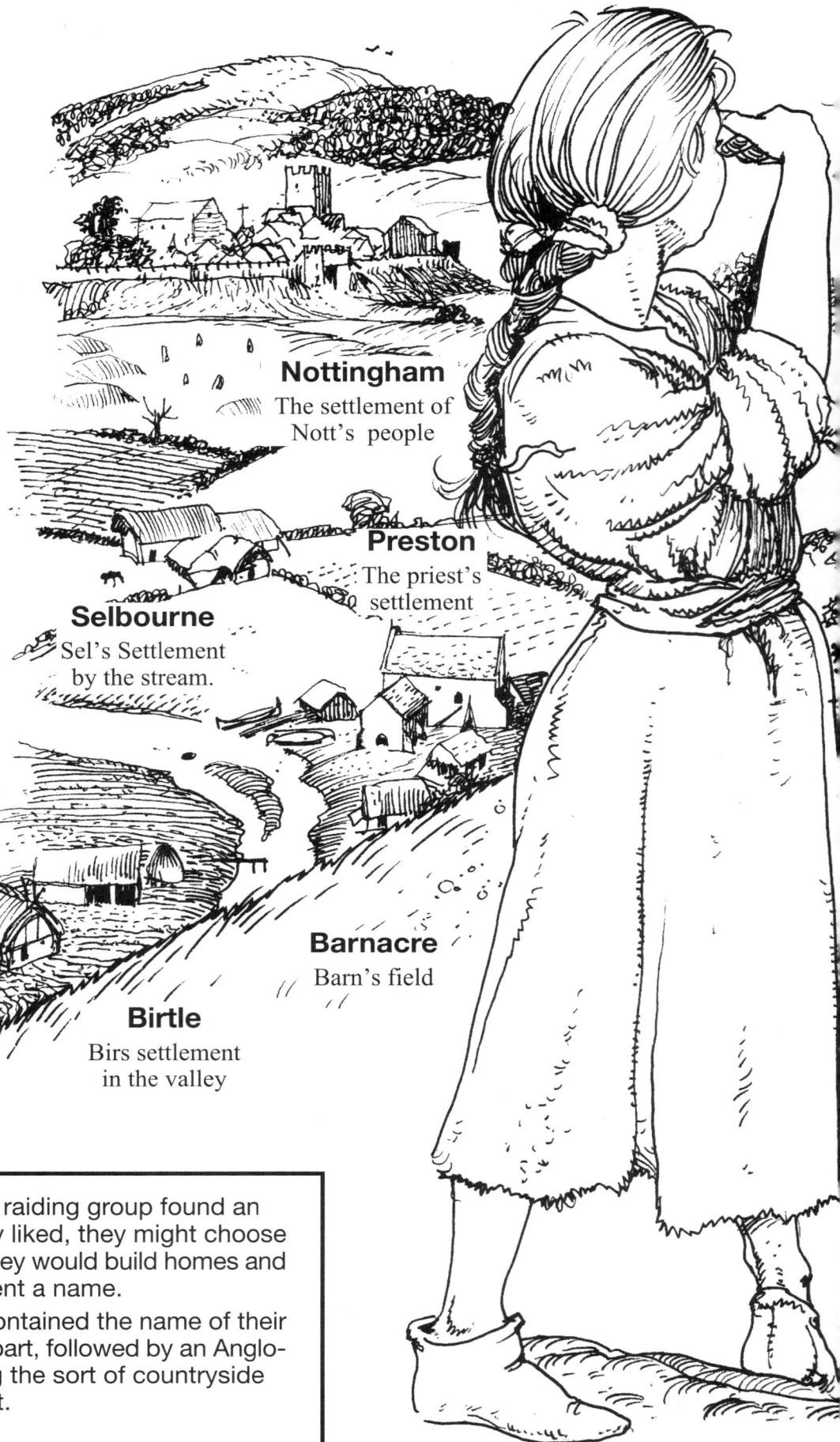

### Anglo-Saxon Describing Words
*(Most of them are suffixes)*

**-aecer:**
a field

**-brycg:**
bridge

**-broc:**
brook or stream

**-burh -burgh:**
on a
shelf of land

**-burna:**
burn or stream

**-ceping:**
market place

**-cype -kip:**
a place
where wicker baskets
are made

**-holh -gol -gle:**
valley

**-ham:**
a settlement of a
tribe or family

**-inga -ing:**
the people of

**-leah -ley -ly:**
field or clearing
in a wood,

**-teagl -tle:**
tongue of land

**-tun –ton -tone:**
settlement of a
tribe or people

**-wick:**
a place where
goods are sold

**Nottingham**
The settlement of
Nott's people

**Preston**
The priest's
settlement

**Selbourne**
Sel's Settlement
by the stream.

**Barnacre**
Barn's field

**Birtle**
Birs settlement
in the valley

When an Anglo-Saxon raiding group found an area of land which they liked, they might choose to settle down there. They would build homes and give their new settlement a name.

Many of their names contained the name of their tribal leader as its first part, followed by an Anglo-Saxon word describing the sort of countryside around their settlement.

# Some of Our Place Names

**Warwick**
War's market place

**Atherstone**
Ather's settlement

**Bartle**
Bar's settlement on
the tongue of land.

**Northampton**
A settlement of Nort's
people

**Aldeburgh**
Ald's settlement
on the cliff
or shelf of land

**Barnsley**
Barn's field in a
clearing in the forest

### Task A:

From reference works, make up your own list of Anglo-Saxon
leaders' names. Then, using Anglo-Saxon words from the
above list, invent new Anglo-Saxon place names of your
own.

### Task B:

Research in reference works, atlases and maps of Britain to
find places that are of Anglo-Saxon origin. Make your own
list of these towns, complete with the Anglo-Saxon meaning
of the place, written out to explain the origin of the name.

# House

see instructions on page 48

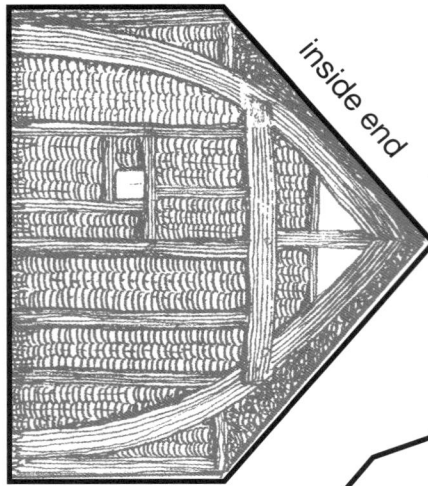

inside end

(see photographs on back cover and drawing on page 19)

roof

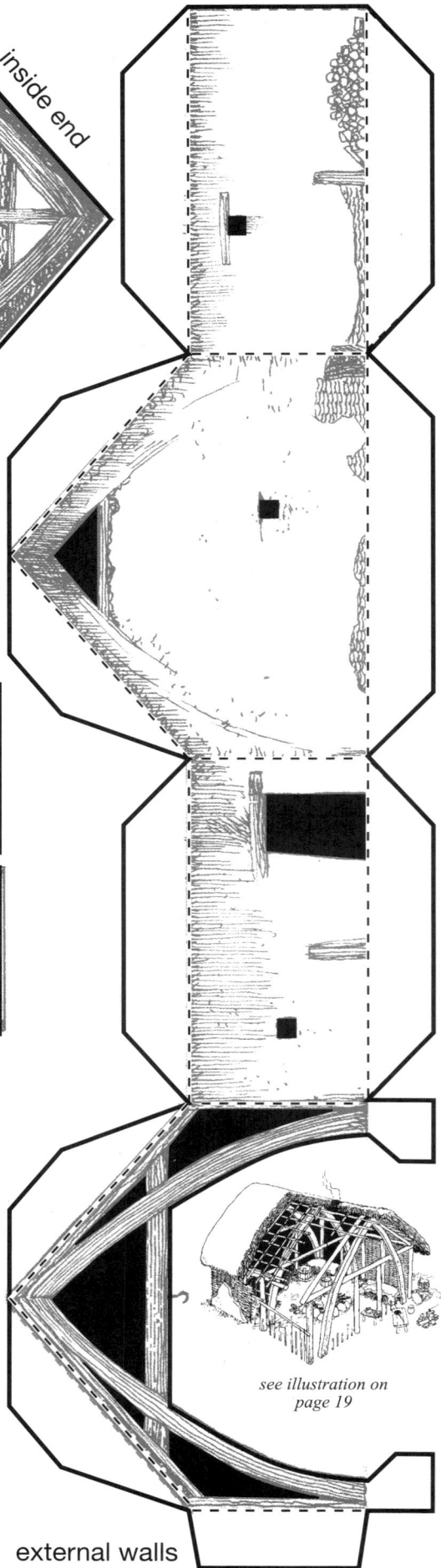

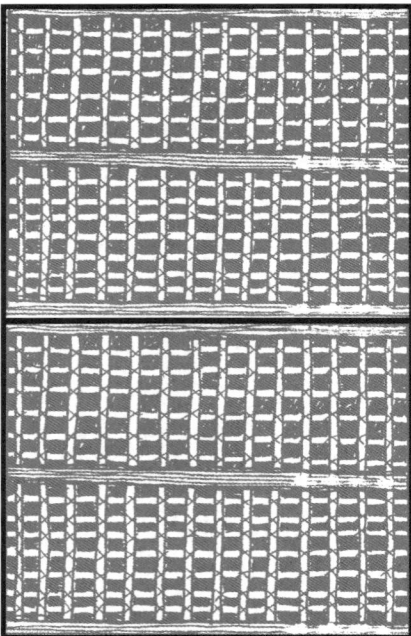

inside roof

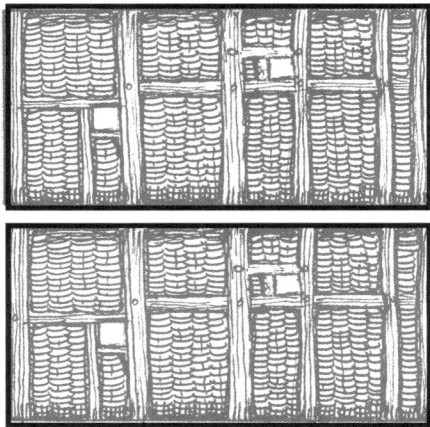

inside side

cut hole for smoke

cut doorway

middle section

fix inside pieces if you wish

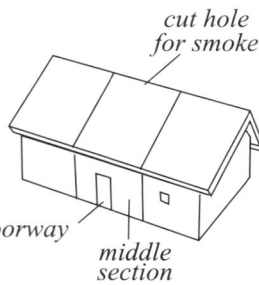

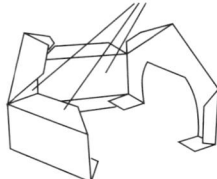

inside floor

see illustration on page 19

external walls

inside wall

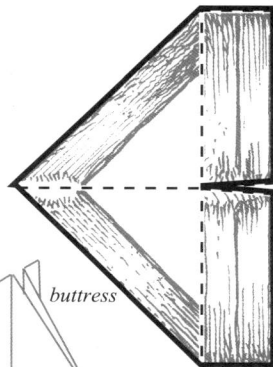

buttress

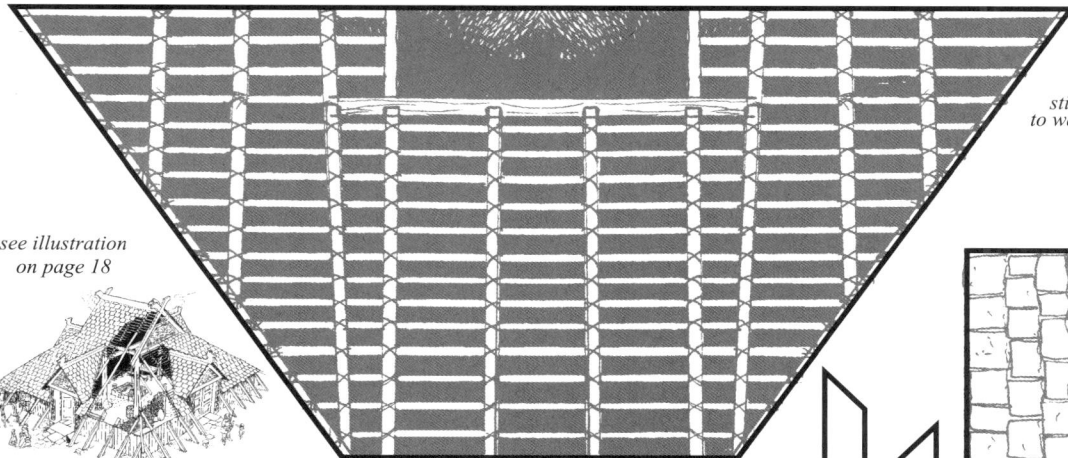

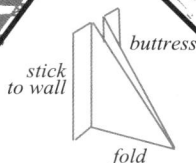

*buttress*

*stick to wall*

*fold*

buttress

roof

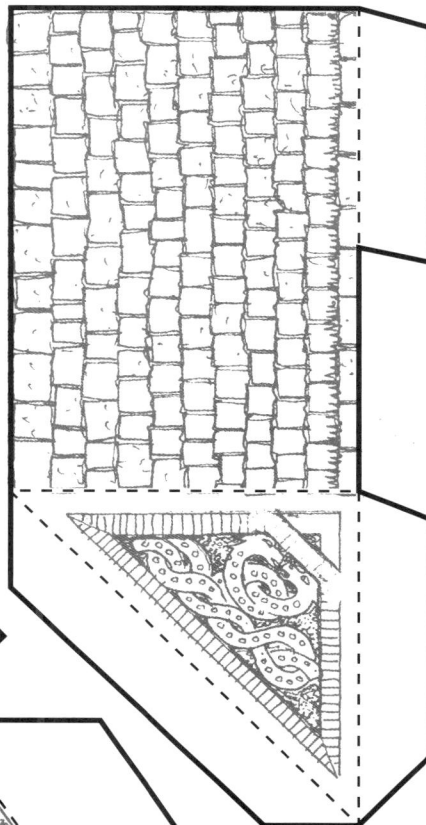

*see illustration on page 18*

inside roof

# Thane's Hall

(see photographs on back cover and drawing on page 18)

see instructions on page 48

entrance

gable ends

buttress

Side wall and roof

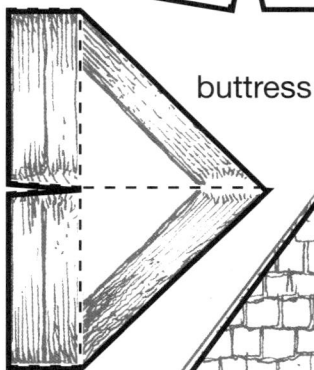

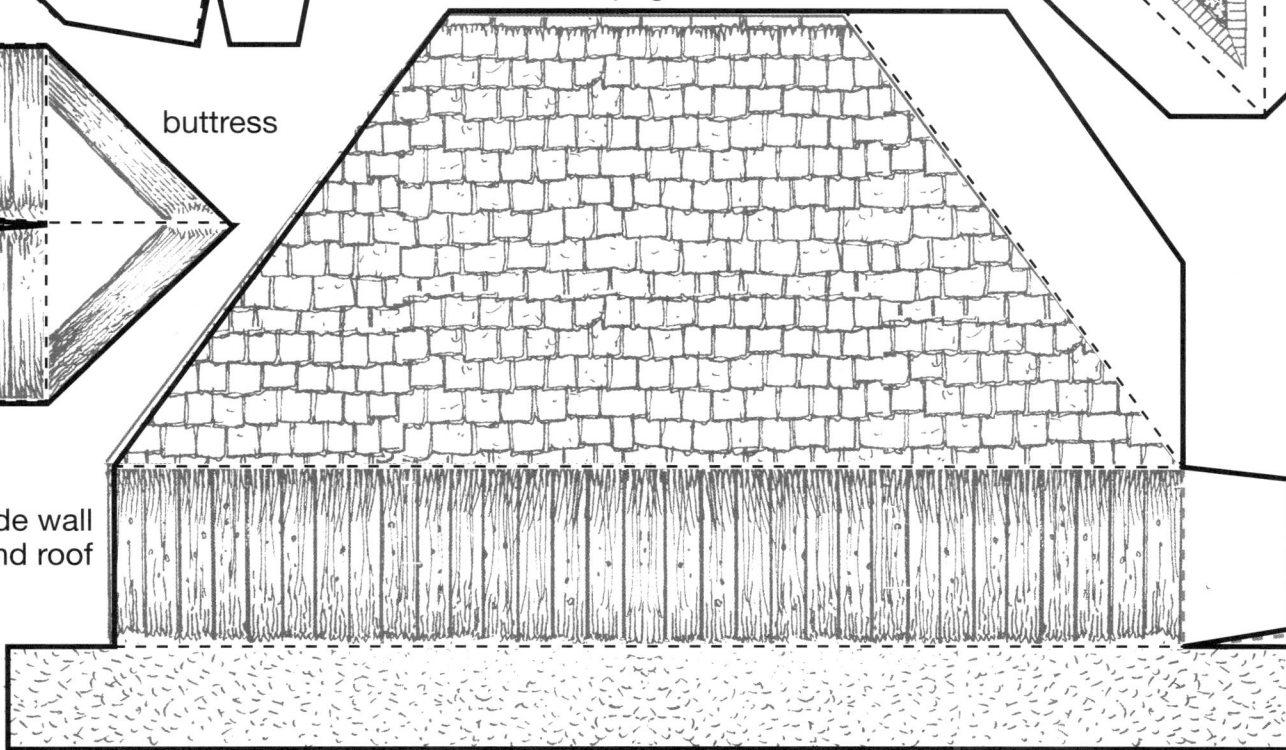

fix to base board

4 photocopies required to make one hall.

buttress

# Church

(see photographs on back cover

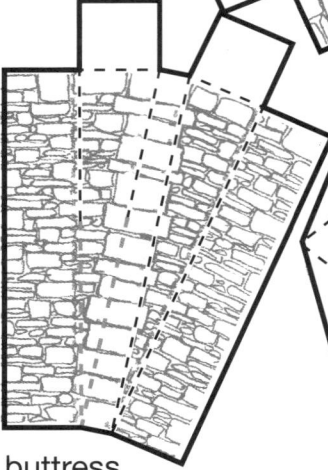

buttress

fix buttress here

fix buttress here

You can see the finished model on the back of the book

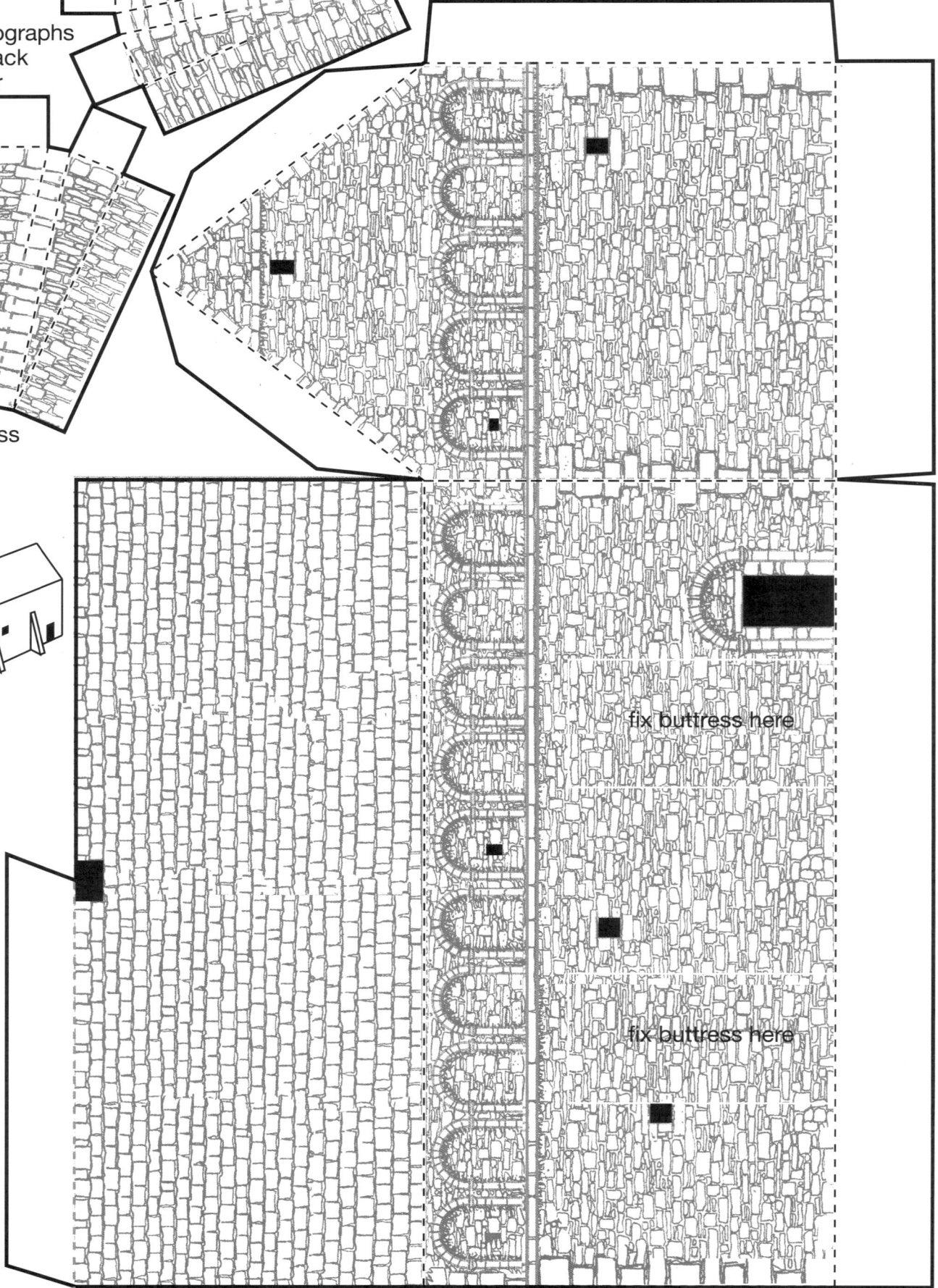

# Helmet

## Sutton Hoo Helmet Instructions:

To make this model impressive and easier to make it should be bigger than it is here on the page. Enlarge the photo copy to A3 at least. it would be better still if the helmet could be made out of gold coloured, thin card.

1  Care should be taken to cut the helmet out. This will require patience. But once cut out the helmet almost makes itself.

2  Using a ruler stroke the eight segments of the helmet to help them to curve.

3  Using glue, sticky tape or a mini stapler, close the segments together to form the conical helmet. The gear teeth-like tabs should be interlocked inside the helmet.

4  The two extensions on the segments either side of the face should be overlapped in front of the face to form the eyebrows and nose protector.

5  The ear protectors should be over-lapped slightly to make them curve, then fixed as indicated.

6  Place the triangular fillets in the neck protector to open the gap and make it flare.

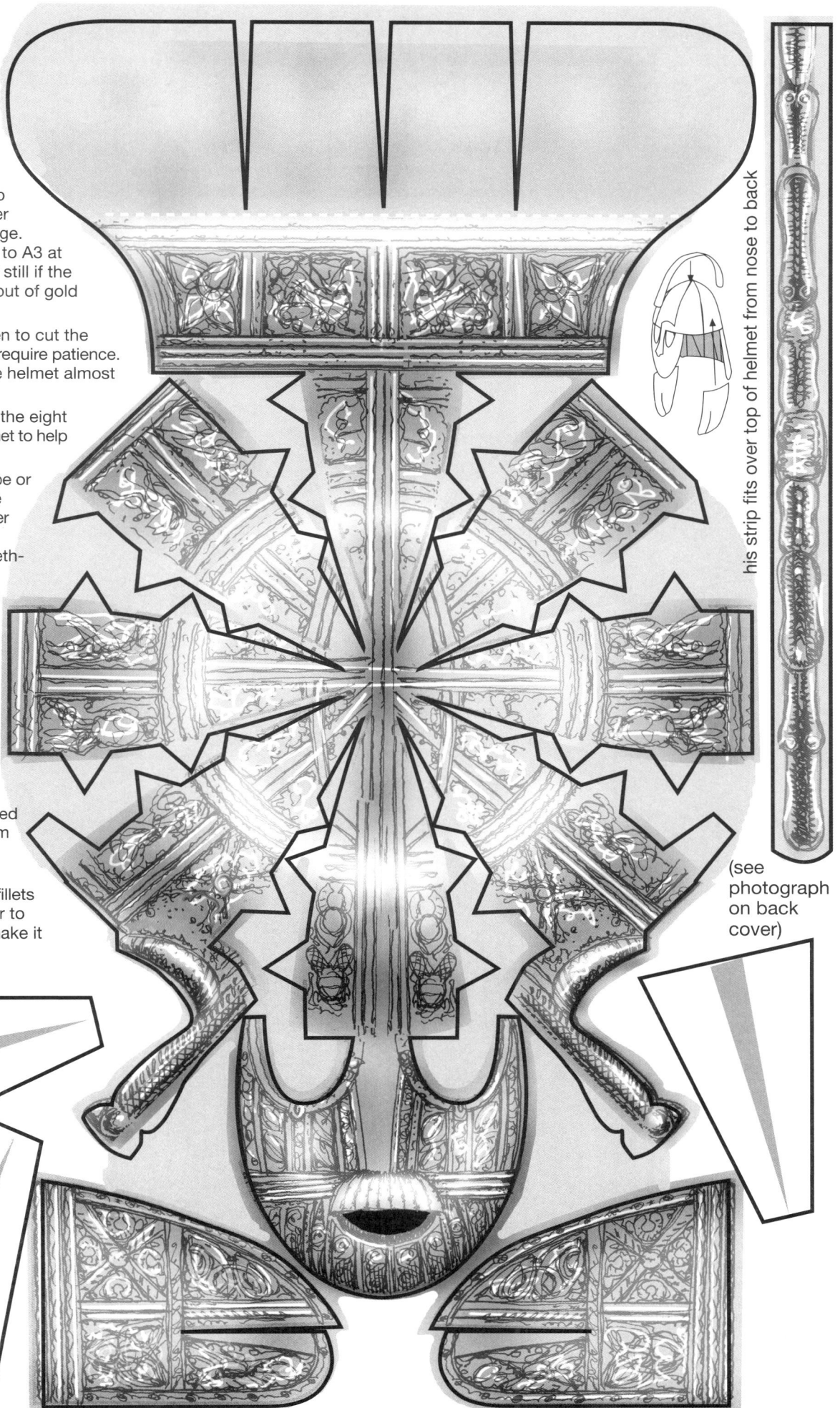

his strip fits over top of helmet from nose to back

(see photograph on back cover)

cut away 3cm of
fence to make
gateway

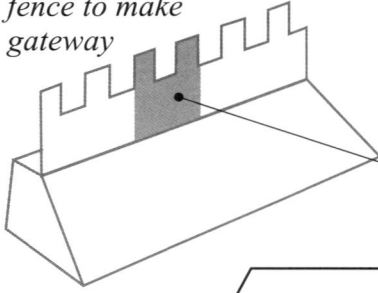

# Wall

## 20 required to complete the circular defensive wall

*Fold and fix together this piece. It will be easier to cut out the battlements after it is stuck together.*
*The shaded area is the section which should be removed on one piece of wall to convert into a gateway.*

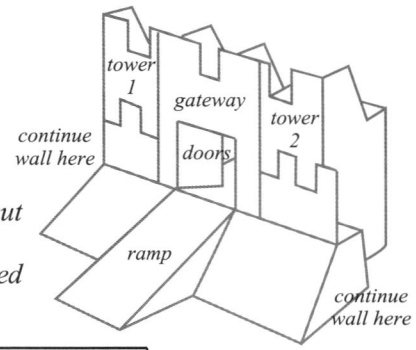

tower 1

gateway

tower 2

continue wall here

doors

ramp

continue wall here

(see photograph on back cover)

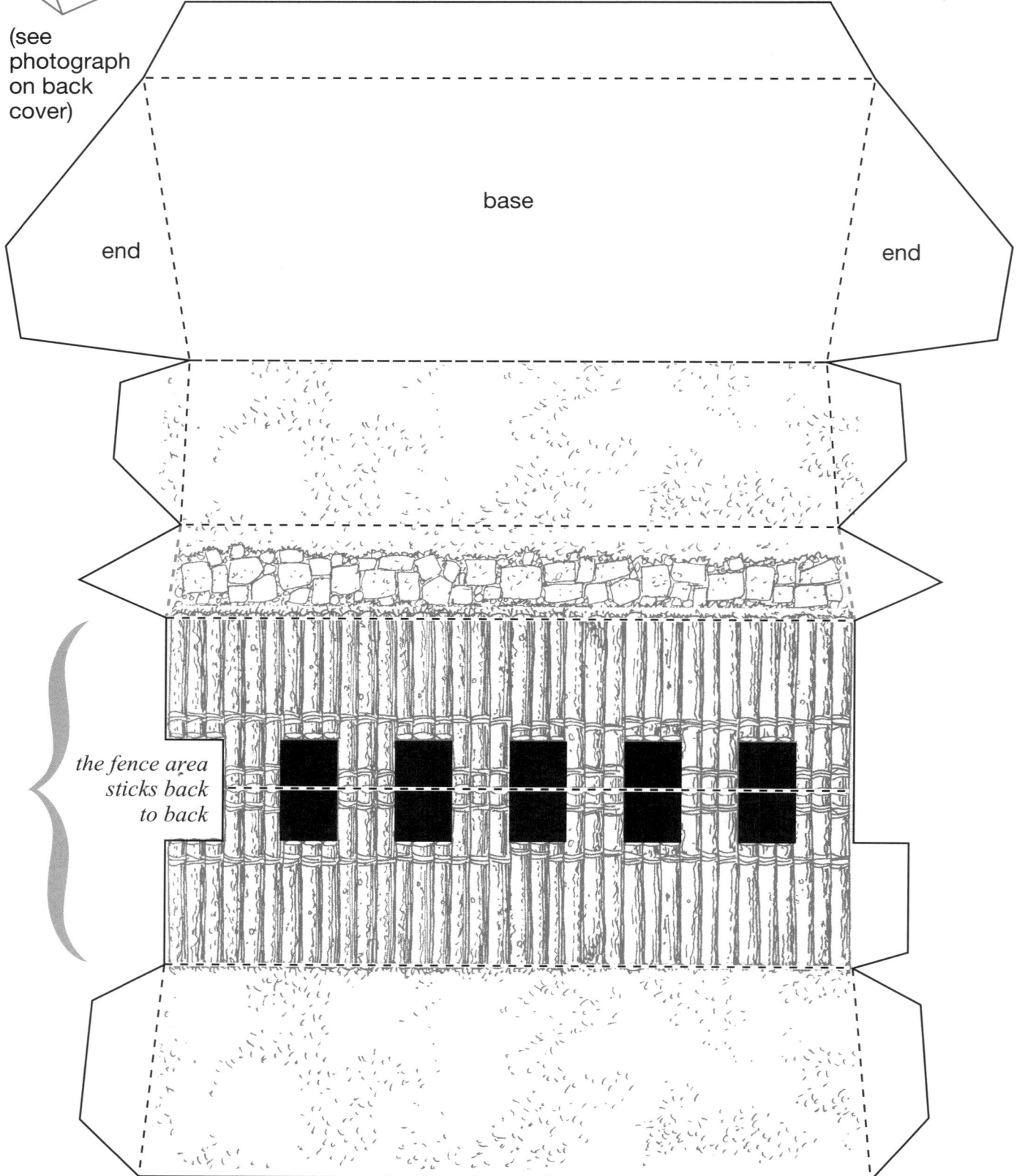

base

end

end

the fence area
sticks back
to back

**Ramp**
(2 required)
(front and
back)

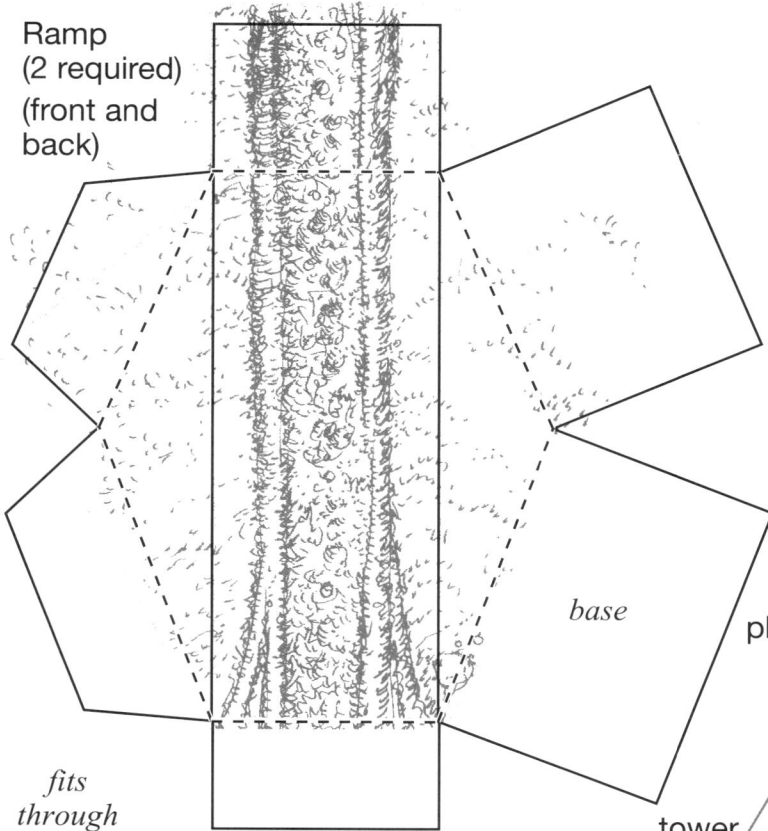

*base*

*fits
through
gate*

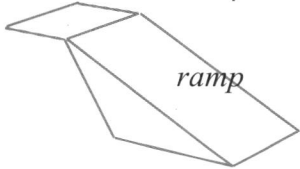

*ramp*

ramp

# Gateway

Gateway

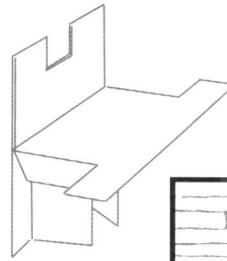

*fits
between
towers*

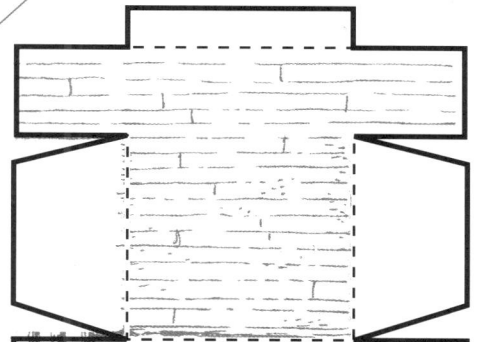

(see
photograph
on back
cover)

tower

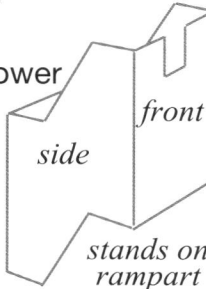

*side*

*front*

*stands on
rampart*

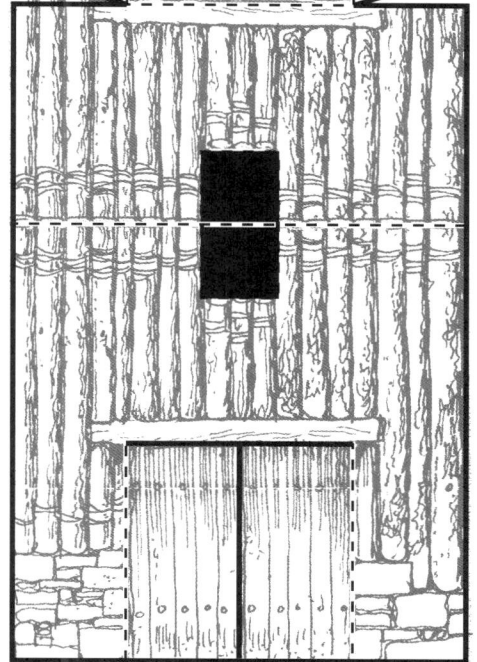

*fold up*

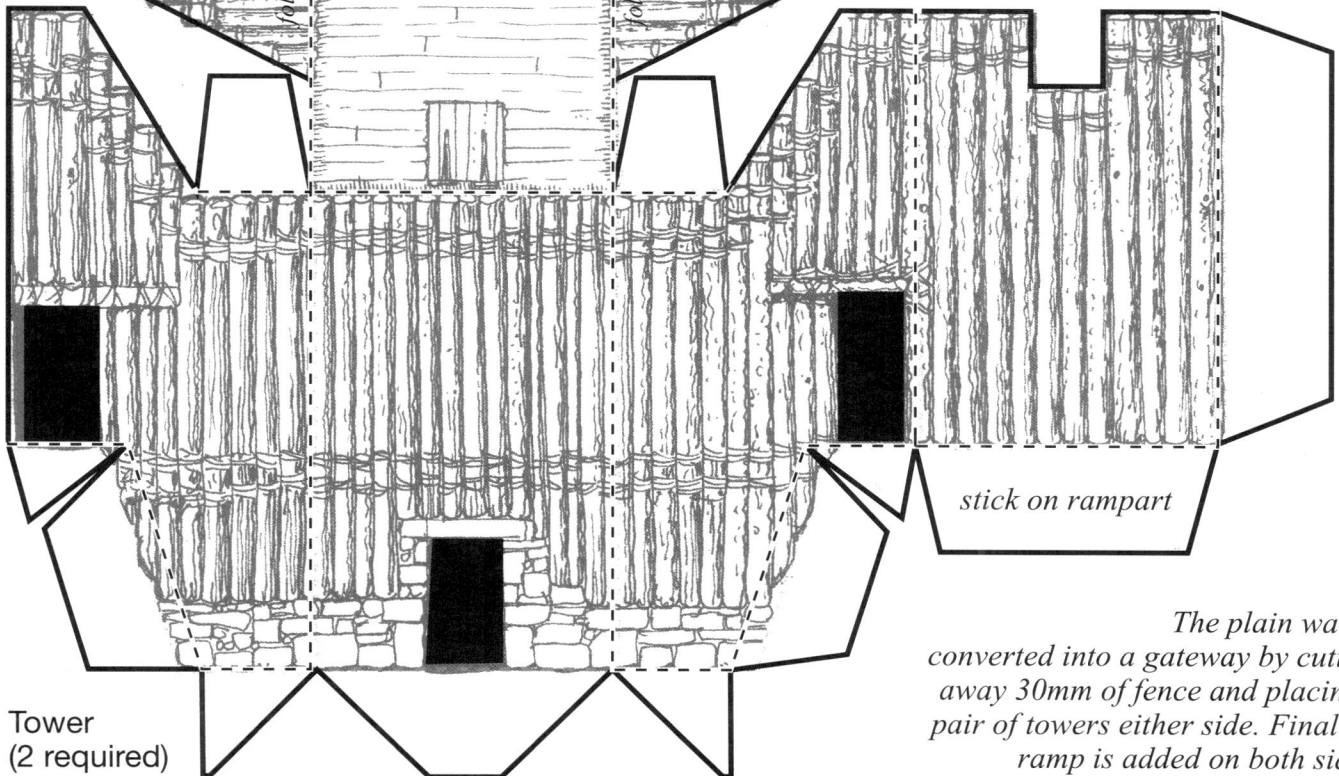

*stick on rampart*

**Tower**
(2 required)

*The plain wall is
converted into a gateway by cutting
away 30mm of fence and placing a
pair of towers either side. Finally a
ramp is added on both sides.*

# Model Instructions

## General:

Decide what size you want to make the models. If you enlarge the models from A4 to A3 they will look more impressive and be easier to make.

If the models are made in thin card they will be easier to make than if they are made from paper. Cream coloured card looks better than white.

If you intend to add colour to the models do this before they are cut out and ideally use crayons rather than paint.

The bold black outlines are to be cut, whilst the grey dotted lines are folding lines. They will fold more precisely and easily if the line are scored first.

### The Models:

The helmet is a complicated model and will require patience to cut out. Once cut out however the helmet is very easy to assemble. The bigger it is, the easier it will be to make.

The church is the easiest model to make. It would make a fine centre-piece to a village.

The house is not difficult. A number of houses would be needed to make a village. The houses could be varied by making them larger and smaller and of different lengths.

The wall is very easy to build. It would surround the village. The ends of the model are at an angle so that if they are placed end-to-end they will form a circular defensive mound. A gateway through the wall should be inserted.

## Church: (pages 44)

To make this model you need two copies of the page 44.

1  Cut out the two pieces which comprise the walls and roof of the church.

2  Assemble the walls and roof and fix to a base board. If you are making the church the same size the base should be 185 x 115mm. If you enlarge it to A3 then the size should be 260 x 160mm.

3  Cut out the 4 buttresses and fix them to the side walls where indicated.

## Helmet: (pages 45)

This model will be more impressive, and easier to make, if it is bigger than on this page. Enlarge the photocopy to A3 at least.

It would be more impressive still if the helmet could be made out of gold coloured, thin card.

1. Care should be taken to cut the helmet out. This will require patience. But once cut out the helmet almost makes itself.

2. Using a ruler stroke the eight segments of the helmet to help them to curve.

3. Using glue or sticky tape on the inside close the segments together to form the conical helmet. The gear teeth-like tabs should be interlocked inside the helmet.

4. The two extensions on the segments either side of the face should be overlapped in front of the false to form the eyebrows and nose protector.

5. The ear protectors should be overlapped slightly to make them curve then fixed where indicated.

6. Place the triangular fillets in the neck protector to open the gap and make it flare.

## House: (pages 42)

To complete the house you need at least two photocopies of the page. One copy will make half the house with an opportunity to see inside. Three or four pieces will make the house longer.

1. Assemble walls of house.

2. Fix inside walls.

3. Fix roof in position. Adjust width of roof if you are adding a middle section.

## Thane's Hall: (pages 43)

To complete the hall you need four photocopies of the page. Each copy will make one side of the hall Leave one side out if you wish to see inside, and if you do, fix the inside walls and roof inside after you have joined the walls together.

1. Join the three or four walls together.

2. Fix down to a base board (If same size, base board should be 170mm square. If A3 base should be 238mm square).

3. Join two sections of roof together.

4. Fix roof on top of hall.

5. Assemble entrance (more than one if you wish) and fix to side.

6. Place buttresses where indicated.

7. Place gable end decorations if you wish.

## Wall: (pages 46 & 47)

The basic wall is on page 46. You will need 20 of these pieces to complete a circular defensive wall. On page 47 are the pieces you will need to convert 1 wall piece to an entrance gate.

1. Cut out the piece on page 46, fold and fix.

2. To convert a wall to a gate first cut away a 30 mm section of wall.

3. You will need 2 copies of page 47.

4. Cut out and fix the towers either side of opening.

5. Cut out ramps and fit. The same ramp is cut differently to fit inside or outside. You need one of each.

6. Cut out gates fold and fit to outside of wall.

## Tree: (below)

Ideally photocopy onto green paper. You will need two copies of the image below to make one tree.

1. Cut out and fold.

2. Fix two pieces together as indicated.

3. Cut away the surplus area around foliage and trunk.

4. Fold and fix base to base board.

*The tree could be copied onto green paper and would compliment the village model.*

# Alfred, The Great Anglo-Saxon King

## Task: Write a Biography

Research in reference books or on the internet to find out as much information as you can about Alfred the Great. You might want to include his burning of the cakes, his defeats by the Viking Danes, his victory over the Danish King Guthrum, his special jewel, his law making and his writings. When you have finished your research then continue the biography and character sketch of Alfred which has been started for you here.

As a child, Alfred loved to hear his mother read the legends of the Saxon kings. His father took the young Alfred to Rome in 855. Alfred loved the riches of Italy and wanted to learn to read the many books in Latin he saw there. But he had no chance to do this as he had to fight for his father against other kings of the different kingdoms of England. He and his brother Ethelred had to fight against the invasions of the Danes, (Vikings from Denmark) every year. In 871 Alfred became King after the death of his brother.

Alfred.......................................

....................................................................................

....................................................................................

....................................................................................

....................................................................................

....................................................................................

....................................................................................

....................................................................................

....................................................................................

....................................................................................

....................................................................................

....................................................................................

....................................................................................

# Anglo-Saxon Gods and Goddesses

**Woden:** Woden was the chief of the gods. He was often shown as a snake to show his cunning. A fierce raven went everywhere with him. Woden could change into many animals. He was very strong so he was sometimes shown as a wild boar.

**Frig:** Frig was Woden's wife, and she was the goddess of the fields and crops. Anglo-Saxons believed she made things grow well. They would pray to her so that they would have plenty of food to eat and lots to drink. Corn and cattle were her symbols.

**Thoren:** Thoren was the god of the sky, and of thunder and lightening. The Anglo-Saxons thought he was very angry when it thundered and lightened. They prayed to Thoren if they wanted to have fine weather.

**Tiw:** Tiw was the Anglo-Saxon god of war. He was shown as a raven or an eagle as they are strong and fierce birds. The Anglo-Saxons prayed to Tiw before they went into battle so that he would help them win their fight.

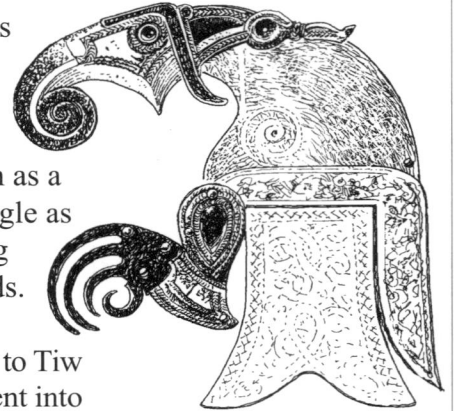

**Nerthus:** Nerthus was a goddess who lived in the woods. She rode about the world on a chariot pulled by fat cows. Wherever Nerthus went in the world, she brought peace and happiness.

**Elves, Dragons and Demons:** The Anglo-Saxons believed that elves, dragons and demons lived in the forests, on the mountains and near waterfalls. They thought these creatures came to pester people who had done something bad in their lives.

# Anglo-Saxon Beliefs

Some Anglo-Saxons buried their kings in ships. They put lots of their belongings like helmets, swords and shields, games, jewellery and clothes in the ground with the dead king. Sometimes they killed a servant or slave and put them with the dead king. Maybe they thought that the dead king would have everything he needed for his new life beyond death.

Other Anglo-Saxons graves have been found without any bodies buried there. Instead Archaeologists have found pottery or metal jars filled with ashes. Some Anglo-Saxons burnt the bodies of their dead, then put their ashes in these jars. Maybe they thought that the dead person's soul went up to a new life with the smoke. They often buried the goods that they thought the dead person would need in their new life in the grave.

## Task A:  Using evidence from pages 50 and 51

1. What evidence tells you that Woden was a strong and cunning god?

2. Why do you think the Anglo-Saxons prayed to Frig?

3. What evidence tells you that Thoren was the Anglo-Saxon god who controlled the weather?

4. How do you know that Tiw was the Anglo-Saxon god of war?

5. Which god do you think the Anglo-Saxons would pray to for happiness and peace?

6. In what sort of places did the Anglo-Saxons think that demons, elves and dragons might pester them?

7. What evidence tells you that the Anglo Saxons thought their dead kings might be travelling on water in their life after death?

8. What evidence tells you that the Anglo-Saxons believed that a dead person lived as a spirit in the next world?

## The Anglo-Saxon god's give us the names of the days of our weeks

**Woden** gives us our name for **Wednesday**.

**Tiw** gives us our name for **Tuesday**.

**Thoren** gives us our name for **Thursday**.

**Frig** gives us the our name for **Friday**.

## Task B

Research in reference works to find out where our names for Saturday, Sunday and Monday come from.

# Different Types of People in Anglo-Saxon England

## Kings

The Anglo-Saxon poem Beowulf tells us that Kings were expected to give their people gold, and to keep them safe from attack. All men had to be ready to fight for their King for 100 days a year.

## Thanes

In the Anglo-Saxon Chronicle Bede tells us that Thanes owned large areas of land. They had to be ready to fight for their king with their people. They had to look after the bridges, roads and forts in their lands.

## Carls

Many Anglo-Saxon poems tell us that Carls were men who were expected to guard their King or Thane. They were expected to fight to the death in battle to keep them safe. They did not do any other work.

## Slaves

In 'The Anglo-Saxon Chronicle', Bede tells us that slaves were people who had been captured in battle. They could be sold like cattle. They had to work hard for no pay, other than their food and shelter.

## Churls

King Alfred wrote a book about all the jobs the ordinary people had to do to grow food for their Thane or King in Anglo-Saxon England. The people had to work very hard. In return their Thane gave them just enough land for them to grow food for their own family. The men had to fight for their Thane for 100 days in a year.

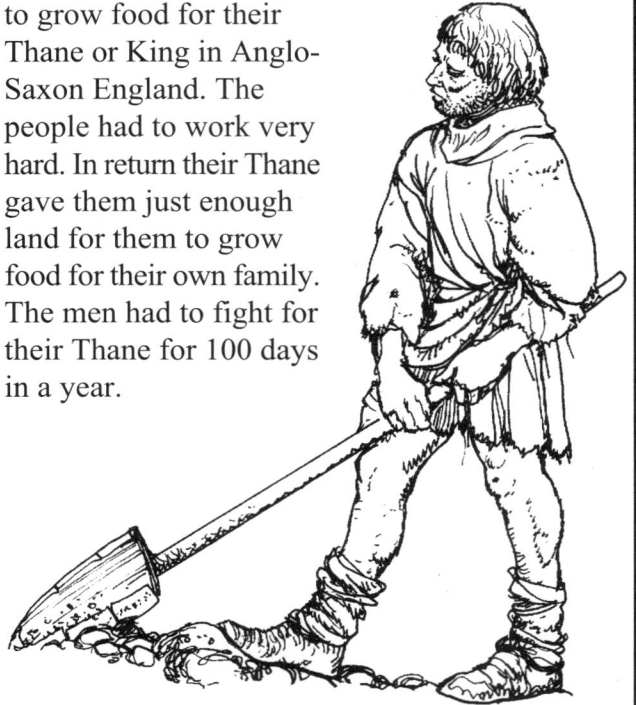

## Task: Interpreting evidence from different sources.

Carefully read the statements below and from the evidence above decide whether each statement is **true**, **false**, or **there is no evidence** for you to decide. Write a reason for your choice to go with each statement.

1. Anglo-Saxon Kings were expected to give their people gold.
2. All men had to be ready to fight for their king for 50 days each year.
3. Thanes had to look after the roads, bridges and forts in their lands.
4. Thanes had small areas of land.
5. Carls had to work hard growing things for their Thane.
6. Carls had to guard their Thanes.
7. Only men could be Churls.
8. Churls were given enough land to grow enough food for their families.
9. Bede wrote about how the Churls lived.
10. Slaves in Anglo-Saxon England got no pay.

# Write a Carl's Diary

## Facts About Anglo-Saxon House Carls

- Saxon House Carls were young men who ate and drank and slept in a chief's hall.

- The Carl's practised fighting each day.

- The Saxon Carls sharpened their weapons every day.

- The Saxon Carls were good horse riders who practised every day.

- The Carls trained by having mock fights with each other.

- If they fought well, their chief would give the house carls a reward.

- The Carls had a shield, a sword, an axe and a spear as weapons.

- The Carls would form a shield wall around their chief in battle to keep him safe.

- The Carls went hunting for deer in the forests, with their chief.

- At night in the chief s house the Carls loved to listen to songs and poems about famous battles.

- The Carls wore helmets and chain mail in battle. They would spend some time each day cleaning their armour.

- The Carls would hope to marry one of the chief's daughters.

### Task: Using Information to Write in a Diary Style

Read the facts on this page carefully and start a House Carls' diary. Research in reference works for further information about Anglo-Saxon chiefs and their House Carls. Use your imagination to complete the diary which has been started below.

## Day 1.

I woke up early. I was excited as today we were going to have a mock battle. Our Chief wanted us to practise our fighting. First, I had to polish my armour and sharpen my weapons. We rode to the edge of the forest to hold our practise battle.

..................................................................................

..................................................................................

..................................................................................

..................................................................................

..................................................................................

..................................................................................

..................................................................................

..................................................................................

..................................................................................

..................................................................................

..................................................................................

..................................................................................

# Make an Anglo-Saxon Brooch

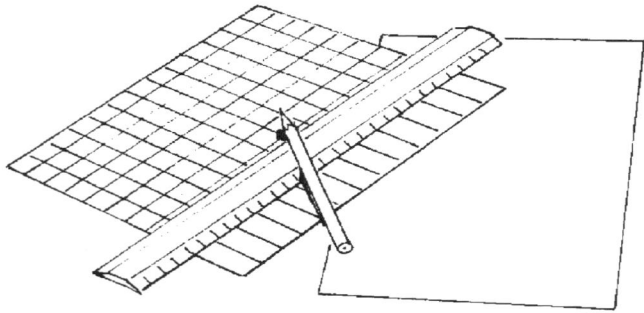

1.  Decide which colours you want to use in your brooch. Using a ruler and pencil, divide different coloured pieces of paper into 5mm. squares

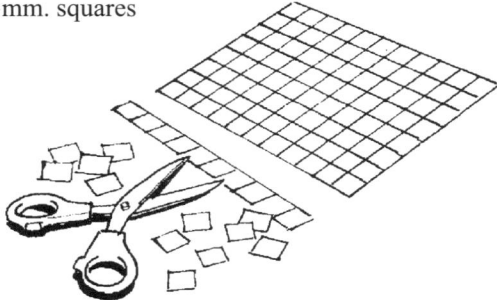

2.  ................................................................
    ................................................................
    ................................................................

3.  Research in reference books to find examples of Anglo - Saxon brooches. Practise a few different designs on scrap pieces of paper or a sketch pad. Remember that the Anglo-Saxon brooches were many different shapes.

### Task A:

Carefully study the pictures and text about how to make an Anglo-Saxon Brooch.
Write your own simple instructions to fill in the missing spaces.

### Task B

Now follow your instructions to make your own Anglo-Saxon brooch. The designs below may help your ideas.

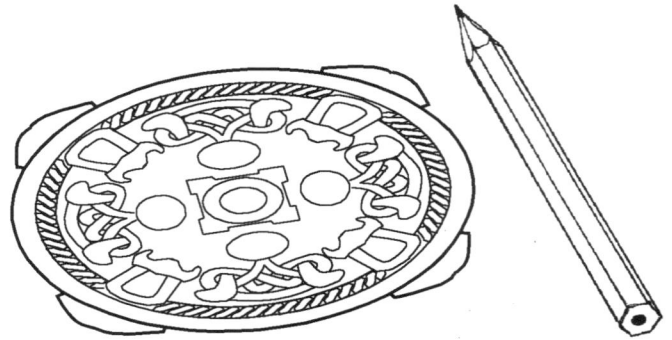

4.  ................................................................
    ................................................................
    ................................................................

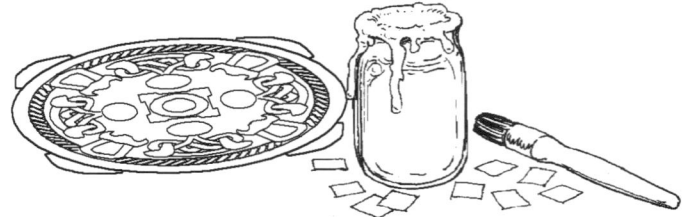

5.  Now, carefully paste the coloured squares onto the correct places on your brooch design. Work steadily until all your design is covered.

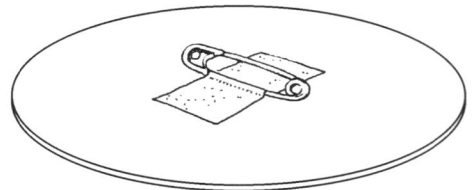

6.  ................................................................
    ................................................................
    ................................................................

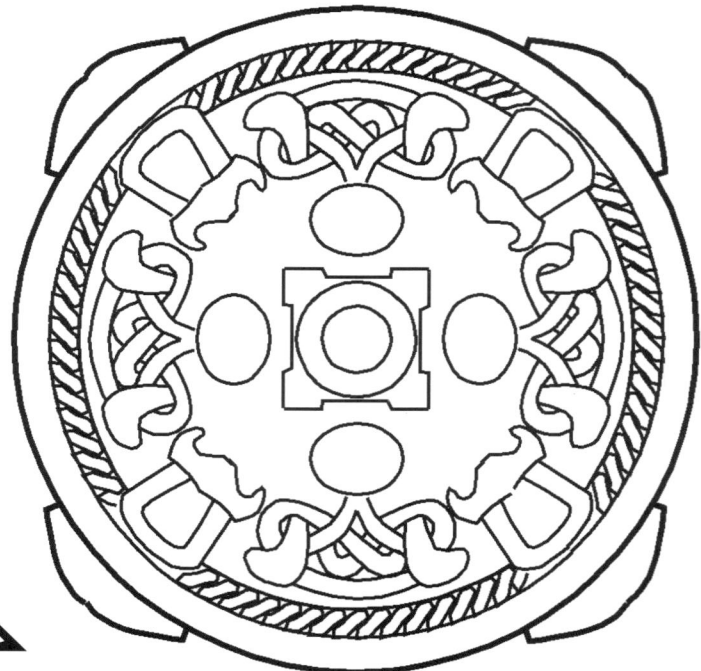

# Paint a Picture of an Anglo-Saxon Fort

# How the Anglo-Saxons Settled in England

About 450 AD the Roman Britons asked the Anglo-Saxons Hengst and Horsa to help them fight off invaders.

Hengst and Horsa told other Anglo-Saxons that there was lots of good land in England.

In their land there was not enough room for all the Anglo-Saxons to have their own farms.

So the chiefs sailed to England to find space for new farms for their people.

The chief would try to find a place on a hill near a river to build their new homes.

Some Saxon chiefs fought the Roman Britons and took over their towns and homes.

1. About 450 AD  the _ _ _ _ _  Britons  asked the _ _ _ _ _ - _ _ _ _ _ _, Hengst and Horsa to help them fight off invaders.

2. Hengst and _ _ _ _ _ told the other Anglo-Saxons that there was lots of good _ _ _ _ in _ _ _ _ _ _ _ .

3. In their _ _ _ _ there was not _ _ _ _ _ _ room for all the Anglo-Saxons to have their own _ _ _ _ _.

4. So the chiefs _ _ _ _ _ _ to England to find _ _ _ _ _ for new farms for  their _ _ _ _ _ _ .

5. The chief would _ _ _ to find a place on a _ _ _ _ near a river to build their new _ _ _ _ _.

6. Some Saxon  chiefs _ _ _ _ _ _ the _ _ _ _ _ Britons and _ _ _ _ over their towns and homes.

7. Carefully  draw your own picture of the Anglo-Saxons sailing to England.

LEVEL

# How the Anglo-Saxons Settled in England

About 400 AD, Rome was being attacked by wild raiders from the East. All the Roman soldiers in England were called back to Rome to fight the invaders. This meant that Roman Britons were left alone to face raiders from across the seas.

Some Roman Britons asked Hengst and Horst, Anglo-Saxon chiefs, to come to Britain to help them fight against raiders from the sea. Hengst and Horst and their fighters won battles against the invaders. They saw that there was lots of good land in England for the Anglo-Saxons to come and settle.

In the lands of the Anglo-Saxons there was not enough land for all the young people to have their own farm. So the Anglo-Saxon Chiefs sailed across the seas to England, with their people, to find a place for them to have their own farms.

When they reached England the chiefs looked for a hill near a river to build their village. They did this because they could defend their homes better at the top of a hill, and being near a river they had a water supply as well as a place for their boats. The Anglo-Saxons built a large hall for their chiefs, with the homes for other families near to it. Sometimes they built a wooden fence around their settlement as a defence against enemies.

Some Anglo-Saxon chiefs attacked the towns and then took over the homes of Roman Britons.

## A.

1. When did the Roman soldiers leave England?

2. Who did the Roman Britons ask to help them against raiders from the sea?

3. What did Hengst and Horsa see that there was in England?

4. Where did the Anglo-Saxons build their settlements in England?

5. What did the Anglo-Saxon chiefs build around their houses?

6. Where in England did the Anglo-Saxons chiefs sometimes attack?

## B.

1. Why do you think the young Anglo-Saxons wanted to sail to England ?

2. Why do you think the Anglo-Saxon chiefs built their settlements at the top of hills ?

## C.

Carefully draw and colour your own picture of the Anglo-Saxon settlement at the top of a hill in England.

# How the Anglo-Saxons Settled in England

Sometime around 400 AD raiding bands from tribes such as the Goths, Visigoths and Vandals began to raid the eastern edges of the Roman Empire, seeking treasures found in the cities of the Roman Empire. As these raids came closer to Rome itself, the Emperor called all the Roman legions back from Britain to defend Rome.

At the same time Britain itself suffered raids by tribes from across the English Channel and the North Sea. These raiders would sail up the estuaries of many rivers and set fire to towns, carrying away treasure, money and people to be slaves.

Not many documents have survived from this period, but legend states that some leaders of the Roman Britons wanted to resist these raids. So they invited the famous fighting tribal leaders Hengst and Horst from a part of Germany, called Saxony, to come with their fighting men, and help fight off the raiders from across the seas.

All these Saxon warriors saw that there was lots of good land for them to have in Britain. In Saxony they were short of land for new families as it was their custom that when a father died his land would be split up between his sons, each son only getting a small part of the land. This meant that there were many young men wanting larger plots of land for their families to live on. Soon many Saxon tribal leaders, or thanes as they were called, began to sail to Britain to find larger pieces of land to settle on.

When they arrived in Britain they would sail up the rivers seeking a suitable place for their new homes or settlements. They sought out hill top sites close to the rivers as these were more easily defended, and were close to a source of water. The tribes would then set up their settlement of small wooden houses around a large wooden hall for their thane. Often they would build a wooden fence for their protection around their settlement. Some Saxon tribes took over Roman British towns as their new tribal home, but even more raided these settlements for the rich objects and money they provided for the tribe's treasure chests.

After many years of Saxon settlement in Britain, the Roman Britons were pushed out of their homes. They moved further and further away from the new invaders, settling in Cornwall and Wales.

## A.

1. Why do you think the Goths and Vandals raided the Roman Empire?

2. Why did the Roman Empire call the legions from Britain back to Rome?

3. What did the raiders do when they arrived in Britain from across the North Sea and English Channel?

4. Why do you think that some Roman Briton leaders invited Hengst and Horst to Britain?

5. Why do you think that there wasn't so much land to share out in Saxony?

6. What did the Saxon settlers build in their new settlements in Britain?

7. Why were the Saxon villages built on hill tops near rivers?

## B.

1. What evidence tells you where Hengst and Horst came from?

2. What do you think a 'legend' is?

3. Why do you think that the Saxon thanes settled in Britain?

4. What evidence tells you why the Roman Britons invited Hengst and Horst to Britain?

5. Why was it that the Roman Britons went to live in Wales and Cornwall?

## C.

Carefully draw and colour your own picture of a Saxon hill top village.

 **LEVEL 4**

# How the Anglo-Saxons Settled in England

In Anglo-Saxon folk lore there is a traditional story of two brothers, Hengst and Horst. Sailing from the tribal homelands of the Angles and Saxons in north western Germany, they helped the tribal leaders of Roman Briton, to fight off other tribes from the east who were seeking to invade the rich island of Britain. The Anglo-Saxon Chronicles written by the Northumbrian monk Bede 863 A.D. relate how the tribes from north western Germany came to settle first in the areas we know as Kent, and East Anglia around 400 A.D., and later to spread their settlements throughout all of what we now call England. The tribes came at the invitation of local Roman British chieftains who wanted the fierce fighting Anglo-Saxons to help them ward off the attacks of many raiders from the continent of Europe. These raiders were exploiting the weakness of the tribes in southern Britain after the Roman legions had left the British Isles. The Roman Emperor needed the legions to help with the defence of Rome, which was being threatened by attacks from the east by wild hordes of Goths, Visigoths and Vandals.

Having battled in defence of the Roman Britons the leaders, or Thanes as the Anglo-Saxon tribal leaders were called, decided that the rich and fertile lands of Britain would provide ideal living space for their peoples. The Anglo-Saxon people had a tradition that on the death of a thane, his lands were to be split up equally amongst his surviving sons. This meant that after a few generations the people were living on smaller and smaller pieces of land, so any chance of gaining more or richer land for their tribes was seized on by these Anglo-Saxons thanes. A relatively short sail across the North Sea or the English Channel, then a cruise up some river estuary led these invaders and settlers to the sites that were to form their new homes.

Tribal leaders would seek some hill top close to a water source or river for their settlement. In the wooded landscape building materials for the tribal hall and small homes was readily available as were the fencing materials for their defensive wall. Alternative settlements were the Roman Briton's towns. The Anglo-Saxon thanes would battle for these rich settlements and force out the native occupants. With many different tribal invasions the settlements of the Anglo-Saxons moved westwards and northwards. Warfare between the tribes, as they established their territories, led to alliances being formed under the strongest leaders, and gradually over a period of a few centuries, separate kingdoms were created in England. In this way the Anglo-Saxon kingdoms of Anglia, Kent. Wessex, Mercia and Northumbria were formed. The kings of these separate regions tended to make their capitals in towns which had formerly been legionary head quarters for the Roman legions, as they were linked to many other places by roads, and were usually already fortified.

A further consequence of this inter-tribal warfare was that the Roman British tribes and people were pushed further and further westward and northward eventually creating separate kingdoms for their tribes in the regions we know as Cornwall and Wales. Alliances and battles between the kingdoms of Anglo-Saxon England gradually led to one kingdom triumphing over the others until Alfred, King of Wessex, became first king of a England, uniting the Anglo-Saxons against the next wave of invaders, the Vikings. Our word England is formed from Saxon words for 'Land of the Angles'.

## A.

1. Why do you think that Hengst and Horsa were invited to Britain?

2. Who do you think wrote the Anglo-Saxon Chronicles?

3. Can you explain the Anglo-Saxon tradition following the death of a Thane?

4. Which areas of England were settled first by the Anglo-Saxons?

5. Why do you think the Roman Britons came to live in Wales and Cornwall?

6. What two factors do you think created the Kingdom of England?

7. Can you explain how the Roman Britain came to be called England

## B.

1. What evidence tells you that the story of Hengst and Horsa may not be true?

2. Why do you think that the Roman Britons invited the Anglo-Saxons to Britain?

3. Why do you think the Anglo-Saxons chose a place near a river for their settlements ?

4. Define the words 'invaders' and 'settlers'.

## C. Use reference works to research:

1. The work of Bede, the historian, of the Anglo-Saxons.

2. One of the five different Anglo-Saxon kingdoms in England.

# The End of the Anglo-Saxon Era

In 1065, when King Edward the Confessor died, Harold Godwinson said that he was King of England.

William of Normandy wanted to be the next King of England. He got his army ready to sail to England in 1066.

Harald Hardrada, King of Norway, also wanted to be the next King of England. He got his army ready to sail to England.

Harold Godwinson beat Harald Hardrada and his Viking army at the Battle of Stamford Bridge near York in 1066.

William of Normandy landed with his army in England. Harold Godwinson rushed with his army to fight William.

Harold was killed at the Battle of Hastings and William became King of England in 1066.

1.  In_ _ _ _, when King Edward the Confessor _ _ _ _, Harold Godwinson_ _ _ _ that he was King of _ _ _ _ _ _ _ .

2.  William of _ _ _ _ _ _ _ _ _ wanted to be the_ _ _ _ King of England. He got his_ _ _ _ ready to sail to England in 1066.

3.  Harald Hardrada, King of _ _ _ _ _ _ also wanted to be the_ _ _ _ King of England. He got his _ _ _ _ ready to sail to _ _ _ _ _ _ _ .

4.  Harold Godwinson_ _ _ _ Harald Hardrada, and his Viking_ _ _ _ at the Battle of Stamford Bridge near _ _ _ _ in 1066.

5.  William of Normandy_ _ _ _ _ _ with his army in _ _ _ _ _ _ _ . Harold Godwinson _ _ _ _ _ _ with his army to _ _ _ _ _ William.

6.  Harold was _ _ _ _ _ _ at the Battle of Hastings and _ _ _ _ _ _ _ became King of England in _ _ _ _.

7.  Carefully draw and colour your own picture of 'The Battle of Hastings'.

**LEVEL 2**

# The End of the Anglo-Saxon Era

King Edward the Confessor had promised that Harold Godwinson would be the next King of England after him. So, Harold was made king in January 1066. However, Duke William of Normandy believed that Harold Godwinson had promised to let him become the next King of England. King Harald of Norway also thought that he should be the next king of England.

King Harald of Norway sailed to England with a large army of Viking soldiers, landing near York. King Harold Godwinson rushed from the south of England, with his army, to do battle with the Viking king. Harold Godwinson beat the Viking army and killed King Harald of Norway at the battle of Stamford Bridge.

Duke William of Normandy then sailed with a large army from France and landed near Hastings on the south coast of England. Harold Godwinson now rushed his army from the battle of Stamford Bridge over 200 miles to face the new threat.

After a fierce battle, William's army slew Harold Godwinson, winning the Battle of Hastings in 1066. From then on, the Normans ruled England instead of the Saxons.

**A.**

1. What did King Edward the Confessor promise Harold Godwinson?
2. Which town did King Harald of Norway land near?
3. What happened at the Battle of Stamford Bridge?
4. Where did Duke William land with his army?
5. What did King Harold Godwinson do after the battle of Stamford Bridge?
6. What sort of battle was fought at Hastings?

**B.**

1. Why did Duke William think that he should be the next King of England after Edward?
2. Why did Harold Godwinson think he was the rightful King of England after Edward?

**C.**

Carefully draw and colour your own picture of the Battle of Hastings in 1066.

# The End of the Anglo-Saxon Era

When Edward the Confessor was made King of England in 1043, he made Norman princes his advisors. The Saxon Godwinson family who ruled Wessex plotted to get rid of the Norman princes. They forced Edward to marry their sister, Edith, and soon they ruled over England as Edward's advisors. Edward resorted to a life of prayer and confession, from which he got his title. Harold Godwinson was sent to Normandy as an envoy for King Edward. Whilst he was there Duke William of Normandy tricked him into swearing an oath that Duke William was to be King of England after Edward's death.

When Edward the Confessor died in January 1066, Harold Godwinson was made King of England immediately. William of Normandy hearing the news began to prepare ships and men for an invasion of England. At the same time in Norway, Harald Hardrada was preparing a fleet of 300 ships to invade England. He claimed that he was the rightful King of England because he was descended from King Knut. He had a huge and powerful army of Viking warriors who were feared throughout Europe. Harald Hardrada sailed across the North Sea and landed in Yorkshire on 8th September 1066. He set off to attack York. On hearing this news King Harold of England summoned his army from the south coast of England, where they had been watching for Duke William's fleet arriving from Normandy, and rode to confront the Viking army. On 25th September, Harold's Saxons defeated and massacred the Vikings at the battle of Stamford Bridge near York. Resting after the battle, they heard that William and his army had landed at Pevensey on the south coast of England. King Harold's army rode south to confront the Normans. On 13th October a battle was fought on a hillside outside Hastings. At first it looked like the Saxons would prevail, but Duke William ordered the archers to fire into the eyes of the Saxons. Legend has it that Harold was shot in the eye. He died on the battle field and his army fled. William became King of England, although it took him many years to conquer the whole country.

## A.

1. Why do you think the Godwinson family plotted against the Norman princes who were advising Edward the Confessor?

2. Where did Harold Godwinson meet William Duke of Normandy?

3. What happened to Harold Godwinson during his stay in Normandy?

4. What was the size of Harald Hardrada's fleet?

5. How do you know that Harald Hardrada's Viking Army were heavily defeated at the Battle of Stamford Bridge ?

6. How do you think Harold's English army were feeling before the battle of Hastings?

7. Why do you think William of Normandy is called the Conqueror?

## B.

1. What evidence tells you that William of Normandy did not always tell the truth?

2. Where was King Harold when he heard that Harald Hardrada and his Viking army had landed in England?

3. Why do you think that the Saxon army had been guarding the south coast of England?

4. What evidence tells you that William was used to giving orders in battle?

5. What evidence tells you that we do not really know how Harold Godwinson died?

## C.

Carefully draw and colour your own picture of the death of King Harold at the Battle of Hastings..

 **LEVEL 4**

# The End of the Anglo-Saxon Era

King Edward the Confessor had spent much of his youth in Normandy. He admired the Norman ways, and when he was made King he brought many Norman nobles to his English court. The Saxon princes, chief of whom were the Godwinson family who controlled Wessex, disliked the Normans and forced the weak Edward to expel them from his court. So that they had more power, they made Edward marry Edith Godwinson. From about 1053, Harold Godwinson was King Edward's chief advisor. King Edward turned to a saintly life of prayer and confession of his sins. Harold went as Edward's envoy to the court of Duke William of Normandy. Unfortunately the ship carrying Harold and his retinue were blown off course, landing in the territory of the Dukedom of Brittany. William paid a ransom for the release of Harold and his party, which made Harold indebted to William. Duke William used this indebtedness to trick Harold into promising that he, William, was the rightful successor to King Edward as King of England. When Harold Godwinson returned from Normandy he found that his brother, the fiery Tostig Godwinson, who was jealous of Harold, had been usurping his power and taking over some of his lands in the north of England. Harold persuaded the weak King Edward to banish his argumentative brother from England. Tostig sought refuge at the court of the immensely strong King Harald Hardrada of Denmark and Norway. He encouraged Harald to prepare to invade England on Edward's death, as King Harold was descended from a previous King of England Knut. On 5th January 1066 King Edward died, and Harold Godwinson was proclaimed King of England. As the news spread, both Harold Hardrada and William of Normandy, prepared their ships and forces for separate invasions of England. On September 20th Harold Godwinson was guarding the south coast of England from a possible invasion by William from Normandy, when he heard that Harald Hardrada, Tostig and their Viking army had landed and beaten local Saxon forces at a battle near York. Harold rushed his army in five days the 200 miles to York. He surprised the army of Harald and in a fierce battle at Stamford Bridge near York, both Harald Hardrada and Tostig were killed and the Viking army routed. Only two days later King Harold Godwinson heard that William had landed on the south coast of England at Pevensey with his invasion force. Harold rushed his men south and on 13th October confronted William's army outside Hastings. A fierce day long battle at close quarters swung first one way and then the other. Harold Godwinson received an arrow wound close to his eye and on seeing this, his fighting house carls lost a little of their courage. Willam led a final charge and the Normans won the battle and England.

## A.

1. Why do you think that Edward was called the Confessor?

2. Why was Harold Godwinson indebted to Duke William?

3. Why do you think Tostig was jealous of his brother?

4. Why do you think Harold banished Tostig?

5. Why do you think that Harold Godwinson's army were at a disadvantage at the Battle of Hastings?

6. What event changed the Batttle of Hastings?

7. Define the terms: 'routed' and 'confronted'.

8. What words do you think best describe the Battle of Hastings?

## B.

1. Define the words: 'ransom' and 'invasion'.

2. What evidence tells you that Harold was not alone when he visited Normandy?

3. What is meant by 'sought refuge at the court of King Harald Hardrada'?

4. What evidence tells you that Harold Godwinson's men were good horse riders?

## C.

Use reference works to research:

1. The Bayeux Tapestry's story of 1066.

2. The weapons used by the three armies in 1066.

# Time to Spare Activities

1. Write a letter to Bede telling him about a Viking raid on an Anglo-Saxon Village.

2. Write a diary of an Anglo-Saxon settler in Britain in 600 A.D.

3. Make a model of the Anglo-Saxon god Woden.

4. Make the inside of a Anglo-Saxon thane's hall from a shoebox.

5. Design and make an Anglo-Saxon shield.

6. Draw a picture of the Sutton Hoo Burial Ship.

7. Research all you can about Anglo-Saxon Kings.

8. Write a diary of an Anglo-Saxon settler's first three days in Britain.

9. Design your own Anglo-Saxon coin.

10. Find out the names of people and places near to you that come to us from Anglo-Saxon times.

11. Draw the objects that Anglo-Saxons might have put in their leader's burial ship.

12. Design and make an Anglo-Saxon belt buckle for your belt.

13. Research as much as you can about King Offa of Mercia.

14. Design your own Anglo-Saxon Burial cross.

15. Make a poster of the different Anglo-Saxon weapons.

16. List the equipment in an Anglo-Saxon kitchen and compare it to a modern kitchen.

17. Make a wall map of the Kingdoms of Anglo-Saxon Britain.

18. Write a biography of Alfred, King of Wessex.

19. Make a poster showing the different events of 1066, at the end of Anglo-Saxon Britain.

20. Design your own Anglo-Saxon interwoven knot border pattern to mount your A4 work sheets within.

21. Make your own poster of Anglo-Saxon pottery.

22. Research as much as you can about the lives of Anglo-Saxon children.

23. Design your own Anglo-Saxon necklace.

24. Choose a year in Anglo-Saxon times and find out all you can about that year.

25. Make your own booklet about Anglo-Saxon women.

26. Make your own page of an Anglo-Saxon illuminated manuscript.

27. Research all you can about the lives of St. Cuthbert and St. Aidan on Lindisfarne island Northumbria.

28. Make your own design for initials for an Anglo-Saxon manuscript.

29. Make your own poster of Anglo-Saxon clothes.

30. Make your own map of Europe showing where the Anglo-Saxons came from and where they settled in Britain.

31. Research all you can about Tostig Godwinson.

32. Write out a list of Anglo-Saxon kings or leaders with their nicknames.